# WHITMAN IN THE LIGHT
# OF VEDANTIC MYSTICISM

*I too have felt the resistless call of myself.*
                                        (Whitman).

*The "I" is below, the "I" above, the "I"*
*behind, the "I" before, the "I" to the right,*
*the "I" to the left; the "I" alone is all*
*this.*

                        (Chhandogya Upanishad).

# Whitman in the Light of Vedantic Mysticism

## AN INTERPRETATION

*by*

## V. K. Chari

With an Introduction by Gay Wilson Allen

UNIVERSITY OF NEBRASKA PRESS · LINCOLN

1964

Copyright © 1964 by the University of Nebraska Press

*All Rights Reserved*

Library of Congress Catalog Card Number: 64-19853

Manufactured in the United States of America

To
my teacher, Professor U. C. Nag,
who helped me to discover Whitman,
*with gratitude and admiration*

# Foreword

In 1856, only a year after the publication of the first edition of *Leaves of Grass*, Thoreau called Whitman's poems "wonderfully like the Orientals," meaning Hindu poems, which Thoreau knew in translation (French, German, and English). On a visit to the poet in Brooklyn, Thoreau asked him if he had read any of the great works of India, and Whitman replied, "No: tell me about them." Exactly what this reply meant is still a matter of controversy, for in "A Backward Glance" (1888) Whitman claimed to have read "the ancient Hindu poems" before writing *Leaves of Grass*.

At any rate, many critical readers of the *Leaves*, from Thoreau to Malcolm Cowley (in his recent Introduction to an edition of the 1855 *Leaves of Grass*), have thought of parallels in Indian literature, especially the Vedantic, while reading Whitman. Swinburne was so reminded while writing his biography of Blake, in whom he found resemblances to Whitman. Edward Carpenter cited parallels between the Upanishads and *Leaves of Grass*. In 1897 William Norman Guthrie stated that in Whitman's poems "Vedantic views are at times expressed with such originality and energy as to have brought a smile of delight to the serene immobile countenance of a Hindu friend, to whom I read them." In 1933 Dorothy Mercer discussed in detail "the teachings of Vedanta" in *Leaves of Grass* and declared that "Song of Myself" is "but an echo of the sayings of Krishna."

In writing my *Walt Whitman Handbook*, I surveyed these comparative studies and for background read such books as were available to me on Vedantic thought and literature. These led me to a paradoxical conclusion about Whitman's mysticism, which seemed most to resemble the Vedantic but was too dynamic to fit the definitions of my authorities. I know now that these were inaccurate and out-of-date in their interpretations of Vedantic mysticism as passive and pessimistic, with the chief goal being nirvana. Today the best scholars of Vedantic idealism insist emphatically that it is not static and passive.

Before Dr. Chari the fault with all studies of Whitman's relation to India has been that they were undertaken by occidentals who did not know enough about Vedantic literature. But that deficiency has now been remedied by a very well-informed and perceptive Indian scholar, the author of the present volume. This study has taught me more than all previous writers on the subject.

The question of Whitman's reading of the "Hindu poems" still remains unanswered, but it is not really important whether he read them or not; whether he absorbed the ideas and attitudes directly, or indirectly, at second or third hand, through American, British, and German Transcendentalism; or—most directly of all—through his own psychology, which enabled him to intuit some of the oldest spiritual truths in human experience.

Dr. Chari wisely does not concern himself at all with sources, which are only of theoretical importance. In this study he is concerned with parallels which have a very practical importance: the Vedantic examples clarify and illuminate Whitman's meaning. This is the only valid excuse for comparative studies, and I find this one particularly helpful. It is useful, too, not only for the Vedantic parallels but also for the argument against Whitman's dualistic concept of the self.

In old age Whitman decided, on superficial grounds, that Hegel was his philosopher, and various critics have tried to trace a dialectic both in his ideas and his poetic techniques. But his concept of the self and selfhood had always been monistic. Like the Vedantic mystic, he found the world in the self, and, as Dr. Chari says, "as the self," thus reconciling "the Me and the Not-Me." In one of his poems Whitman extolled the power of a person to "enter upon all, and incorporate them into himself or herself."*

Dr. Chari's interpretation of Whitman seems to me important not only to Whitman criticism and scholarship but also for any thoughtful person of the Western world today. Here in Whitman and the Vedantic parallels are concrete examples of a healthy, vital philosophy of selfhood much needed in the twentieth century.

* "Thoughts" ["By the Roadside."]

In his prophetic poem "Passage to India," Whitman envisioned man and nature "disjoin'd and diffused no more." The "true son of God," the poet, would fuse them. Despite the title, this poem is not so Vedantic as "Song of Myself," but perhaps it was more prophetic than we Westerners had realized in the poet's call for a return

> To reason's early paradise,
> Back, back to wisdom's birth, to innocent intuitions,
> Again with fair creation.

GAY WILSON ALLEN

# Preface

I have attempted in this study to give a consistent account of Whitman's poetic thought and belief, proceeding from the central standpoint of the self, in which I have sought to discover the key to Whitman's meanings. For me the primary problem of reading Whitman is that of interpretation, though in this, of course, there can be no agreement. But still I believe it is possible to discover in his poems a unifying principle in the preoccupation with the problem of self.

While I have explained this unity of thought and experience in Whitman in purely Vedantic terms, the Vedantic comparison is to be understood simply as a critical instrument—one that I have used to define and illustrate Whitman's most basic ideas. Yet even if we dispensed with the Vedanta we would still have to reckon with the idea of selfhood for any honest interpretation of Whitman. It is possible that this study might seem a little overenthusiastic in its Vedantic application—I might seem to have read more Vedanta into Whitman than another might be willing to admit. But I believe that I have nowhere forced Whitman's meanings.

It must not be supposed that in claiming Whitman to be Vedantic I have denied other, non-Vedantic, strains in his thought, such as his being an American in his poetic origins, as in some of his basic attitudes. For instance, Whitman's dynamism was the legitimate product of a dynamic phase in the life of an expanding continent. If my study makes any claim, it is to a certain inclusiveness of treatment, one aspect of which is to show that the all-embracing quality of Whitman's vision makes possible the existence in it of strands of thinking which, far from being contradictory, may be seen to proceed from a central unity of perception. Thus, Whitman's celebration of the physical and

xi

material is entirely consistent with his celebration of the soul. When I call Whitman a Vedantic mystic I do not deny his claims for being the bard of American democracy. On the other hand, I show that mysticism is the clue to his democratic idealism; we cannot separate his idea of democracy from his conception of selfhood.

I quite realize that this book is burdened with citations from Sanskrit scriptures, with philosophical expositions and niceties of distinction such as may render it difficult reading. But I have tried to put in only as much philosophical exposition as is indispensable for my argument. The distinctions that I have pursued, like those between "dialectic" and "intuition," and Hegel and Vedanta, seemed crucial to an understanding of Whitman's mysticism.

Perhaps this book would not have taken shape had it not been for Professor Gay Wilson Allen's encouragement and sympathetic judgment. Professor Allen accorded me the privilege of several personal discussions with him while I was writing this book, and he very kindly read through my manuscript and offered me much helpful criticism. I owe him a deep debt of gratitude for this and many other personal kindnesses. The manuscript was also read by Professor James E. Miller, Jr., and Professor Bernice Slote, who encouraged me and advised me on putting the work in shape for publication. Professor Miller also supervised the editorial revision of the manuscript, and my obligation to him is great.

I also wish to thank Mr. Malcolm Cowley for the benefit of personal conferences with him and for his helpful comments. And I am grateful to Professor T. R. V. Murti of Benares Hindu University for many a provocative discussion on Vedanta philosophy. My understanding of Vedanta is largely due to him.

I must also acknowledge my general debt to recent Whitman scholarship, particularly to the work of Professor Allen and of Professor Miller. I was much encouraged in my interpretations by Malcolm Cowley's recent defense of "Song of Myself." I owe an obvious debt to such able expositions of the Indian philosophical systems as M. N. Sircar's *Hindu Mysticism: According to the Upanishads*, P. T. Raju's *Thought and Reality: Hegelianism and Advaita*, T. R. V. Murti's *The Central Philosophy of Buddhism*, and to the many profound expositions of Indian philosophy by Professor S. Radhakrishnan. In my own exposition of philosophical ideas, I have generally adopted the argument and even the language of these books. In quoting from the Hindu scriptures I have generally used the English translations by Swami Nikhilananda and S. Radhakrishnan among others.

This study is substantially the text of my doctoral dissertation submitted to Benares Hindu University in 1950, though modified and revised, and I wish to thank this university for permission to publish it. Finally I wish to thank the United States Educational Foundation in India for a Fulbright Fellowship in 1959–1960, and the State College of Education, New Paltz, New York, for an assistant professorship in 1960–1961, both of which made possible a period of research at New York University for the preparation of this book

V. K. C.

Benares Hindu University

# Contents

# CHAPTER ONE

# Introduction:

## Our Approach to Whitman

With the growth of Whitman's reputation in recent decades we have had a superabundance of scholarly writing on him, and the impetus of the centennial year of *Leaves of Grass* has released a further spate of critical and biographical works, outstanding among them Professor Gay Wilson Allen's monumental critical biography *The Solitary Singer*. In the last five or six years alone there have appeared several critical revaluations of the poet, some of which, like James E. Miller's *A Critical Guide to Leaves of Grass*, and *Walt Whitman's Poems*, edited by Gay Wilson Allen and Charles T. Davis, are admirable attempts to discover the aesthetic form of Whitman's poems. The very recent presentation by Malcolm Cowley of the 1855 edition of *Leaves of Grass* is another significant event in the march of Whitman criticism, for it brings into renewed focus certain important aspects of Whitman's poetry. In addition to books there has been a steady flow of journalistic writing.

All this growing mass of Whitman scholarship is proof not only that Whitman's position among the great men of world literature is assured, but also that there is a new awareness of Whitman's poetic worth and a keenness to rediscover value and significance in both his art and his message. Although twentieth-century "highbrow" classicists do not quite approve of "the first white aboriginal," there are signs that Whitman is slowly being reclaimed. This shift in attitude toward poets like Whitman may well be the beginning of a reaction against modern poetry and criticism,[1] but it is also quite clearly an indication of a change in intellectual climate. Thus, the poet Randall Jarrell in *Poetry and the Age* has demonstrated that Whitman's poetry contains many lines of dazzling originality and that of all modern poets Whitman has the most "comprehensive soul." "Whit-

[1] Karl Shapiro, *In Defense of Ignorance* (New York: Random House, 1960).

I

man's poems represent his world and himself much more satisfactorily than Tennyson's do his."[2] Karl Shapiro is perhaps one of the boldest early defenders of Whitman among our contemporary poet-critics. He began his defence of the Whitman tradition as it continues in Hart Crane in his *Essay on Rime*. He saw Whitman's true significance as the poet of "Song of Myself" and not as a national spokesman:

> But who
> Except Hart Crane has tasted the pure manna
> Of *Song of Myself*, the naked seed of rime?
> When Whitman had the nation on his brain
> He served us ill, in my opinion; his leap
> Into the personal infinite, however,
> Saved him from drowning in his Susquehanna.[3]

A full-scale justification of the Whitman tradition is contained in the recent book *Start with the Sun: Studies in Cosmic Poetry*, by James E. Miller, Jr., Karl Shapiro, and Bernice Slote. The authors examine the Whitman tradition, of which the key figures are Whitman, D. H. Lawrence, Hart Crane, and Dylan Thomas, as opposed to the other, more vocal, Eliot tradition. Lawrence, Crane, and Thomas are the "poets of the Kosmos" that Whitman envisioned and are Whitman's spiritual heirs, because they wrote the life-poetry, the affirmative, rather than the negative poetry of the Eliot tradition. The significance of this study is that, besides justifying Whitman's poetic achievement, it focuses attention on Whitman the mystic, the poet of cosmic consciousness. Thus, in the opening chapter Bernice Slote observes:

> That the real Whitman was a mystic, a poet of cosmic consciousness and life-force in all of nature; that he was primarily a religious poet (priest of the New Paganism, perhaps); and that he was a poet of artful control—these things recent criticism is beginning to make clear.[4]

Karl Shapiro, too, emphasizes Whitman's mysticism:

> He is the one mystical writer of any consequence America has produced; the most original religious thinker we have; the poet of the greatest

[2] Randall Jarrell, *Poetry and the Age* (New York: Vintage Books, 1955), p. 115.
[3] *Essay on Rime* (New York: Reynal & Hitchcock, 1945), p. 30.
[4] Miller, Shapiro, and Slote, *Start with the Sun* (Lincoln: University of Nebraska Press, 1960), p. 6.

achievement; the first profound innovator; the most accomplished artist as well. . . .[5]

This is a complete reversal of the attitude represented by the Eliot school. It would seem that something like a new evaluation of Whitman is under way.

An important reason for this revival of interest in Whitman among both academicians and poet-critics is a renewed appreciation of Whitman's value as a mystical poet and a willingness to explore meanings which might have escaped the notice of his antagonists. This interest in Whitman's mysticism is, of course, not new. Starting with Emerson and Thoreau, a long line of enthusiasts and scholars, notably R. M. Bucke and William James, have viewed him as an essentially religious poet. But in our own day there seems to be a pointed emphasis on Whitman's self-oriented attitude, his inclusive vision, and affirmative tone. Perhaps this renewed concern for Whitman as mystic is reinforced by the present-day generation's fascination with Eastern religions; interest in Zen Buddhism has become a considerable force in the intellectual world of the West. Both artists and intellectuals seem to be searching for a confident and affirmative message to restore serenity and fulfilment to a frustrating and confusing world. This search takes the form of a self-quest, a general preoccupation with the questions of the self, of which the existentialist philosophy is but a morbid manifestation. The ancient spiritual tradition of Asia, with its methods of meditation and self-discipline and its exalted conception of selfhood, might be found to promise a cure for much of the modern malaise. In the context of these spiritual needs, Whitman's poetry assumes a new relevance and appeal to our generation. An important aspect of this new Whitman appeal is a recognition of value and meaning in Whitman's mystical songs of the self, hitherto generally censured as "barbarous."

No doubt, there has all along been a rather reluctant admission that the "Song of Myself" occupies a central position in the entire poetic work of Whitman. But the resistance to it and to the other poems comprising the earlier edition has been much stronger. Santayana condemned Whitman as a barbarian, and Bliss Perry, writing his Whitman biography in 1906, complained of the "bathos and vulgarity" of the "turgid, sprawling, extravagant" poems of the earlier *Leaves*,

[5] *Ibid.*, p. 58.

and praised the "poignant realism" and "terrible and tender beauty" of "Drum-Taps" and the "pure beauty" of the death lyrics. This aversion to "Song of Myself," to its apparent formlessness and its blatant egotism, has continued as a dominant strain in Whitman criticism, despite occasional vindications. The rejection of Whitman's cult of "Myself" and his cosmic enthusiasm was completed by T. S. Eliot, who stands in an "antipodean" relationship to Whitman. Eliot had to conquer "an aversion to his form" as well as to what he called the "clap-trap" in his content in order to read him. There were, of course, fundamental temperamental differences between Whitman and Eliot and the poets of Eliot's generation. Eliot was a traditionalist and a Christian who returned to the received bonds and inspirations of religion; Whitman was a heretic who banished the gods and shamelessly installed himself in the pantheon. Eliot believed in the Christian concepts of sin and redemption and perceived the "chasm between the real and the ideal such as opened before the horrified eyes of Baudelaire," a "serious and Catholic Christian," whereas Whitman was essentially "satisfied—too satisfied—with things as they are." Whitman did not perceive that "what really matters is sin and redemption" and hence was incapable of the sense of intense moral struggle. Eliot has remarked: "With the disappearance of the idea of original sin, with the disappearance of the idea of intense moral struggle, the human beings presented to us both in poetry and prose fiction today . . . tend to become less and less real."[6] It is such a disposition that prompted him to see in Whitman's death lyrics the poet's only justification for being. Reviewing Emory Holloway's biography of Whitman more than thirty years ago, Eliot commented, "When Whitman speaks of the lilacs or the mocking-bird his theories and beliefs drop away like a needless pretext."[7]

Modern sensibility (or the "New Puritanism") dwells in the fatal knowledge of its own inexpiable guilt; the problems of original sin, origin of evil, and the like, which Emerson called "the soul's mumps, and measles, and whooping coughs," are its major obsession. It seeks refuge in god-relation and humility and expresses itself in "dialectic irony," which Kenneth Burke has called "the technical equivalent for the doctrine of original sin." It is a decided preference for the tragic

[6] *After Strange Gods* (New York: Harcourt, Brace & Co., 1934).
[7] "Whitman and Tennyson," *Nation & Atheneum*, XL (December 18, 1926), 426.

mode that has provoked Allen Tate to call Emerson "the Lucifer of Concord."[8] According to Tate, Emerson's transcendental doctrine, by identifying man with the oversoul, left no scope for struggle and tragic fault, and without tragic fault there is no drama in human character. Hawthorne alone kept pure the Puritan drama of the soul. Tate quotes Robert Penn Warren as saying, "After Emerson had done his work any tragic possibilities in that culture were dissipated." Emily Dickinson, in Tate's view, was the product of the "perfect literary situation"—which, according to him, arises when a poet strives to live apart from a cultural tradition that no longer sustains him, without at the same time dispensing with it. From this view, Whitman's complete repudiation of tradition would rob him of the benefit of "tension" and "polar activity" which provide the poet with this perfect literary situation. Whitman, as Eliot has complained, was too satisfied with things as they are; he could not feel the agony of a culture. In his cosmic appetite he not only swallowed the universe like a cake but transmuted the ideal into the real with a prodigious facility. His poetry perpetuates the worst kind of make-believe. So here is the great divergence of attitude that separates Whitman from the tradition that runs from Hawthorne and Melville through Eliot.

Even today Whitman's critics do not seem to have quite overcome their aversion to the "barbaric yawps" of "Song of Myself." No wonder, therefore, that even the more friendly of them have constantly turned to his "sea-shore lyrics" and elegiac poems for a justification of the poet. Thus, a recent estimate says: "It is not to the life-affirmer we are returning, but to the elegiac Whitman, the poet of death."[9] The prevailing scholarly opinion today, though it is not completely blind to the merits of Whitman's earlier poems of the "Song of Myself" category, still seems to be that Whitman's death lyrics are the high-water mark of his poetic achievement, and that the poet got over the arrogance and turgidity of his early verse and matured and deepened into the finer sensibility and lyric power of "When

[8] See Tate's essay on "Emily Dickinson" in *The Man of Letters in the Modern World* (New York: Meridian Books, 1955).

[9] Leslie Fiedler, "Images of Walt Whitman" in Milton Hindus, *Leaves of Grass One Hundred Years After* (Stanford, Calif.: Stanford University Press, 1955), p. 72. Roy Harvey Pearce also thinks that Whitman may be best justified as a poet by the 1860 edition, according to him the most important edition of *Leaves of*

Lilacs Last in the Dooryard Bloom'd." It is quite legitimate to hold that the "sea-shore lyrics" and the "Lincoln elegy" mark a new depth in Whitman's verse. As Professor Allen contends, Whitman's art underwent mutations through successive editions and often revealed unmistakable growth in terms of a more deliberate control of material.[10] What needs to be made clear, however, is that the later poems, the elegies and the short poems, certainly among Whitman's finest lyrics, are different from, though not necessarily superior to, "Song of Myself."[11] While we do not question the artistic merit of these lyrics, it is debatable whether in judging Whitman's poetic

---

*Grass*, and its most important poem "Out of the Cradle." The 1855 and 1856 editions are seen as stages on the way to the maturity of the 1860 edition. "Whitman justified," in *The Presence of Walt Whitman*, ed. R. W. B. Lewis (New York and London: Columbia University Press, 1962), pp. 72–109. Stephen Whicher ("Whitman's Awakening to Death," *ibid.*, pp. 1–27) dwells on Whitman's awakening to the vision of death—"the demonic underside of Whitman's vision"—which remained a permanent part of Whitman's truth. Thus it is a troubled night-consciousness or dark under-consciousness that he treats in "The Sleepers," not the expansive bardic vision of "Song of Myself." Whicher argues that the dark element, the obsession with death, is as strong in Whitman from the beginning of his work as his other element of transcendental joy, though sometimes it was dominant and at other times recessive. The view that I have consistently maintained in this book is that whereas the theme of death runs through all of *Leaves of Grass* it is rather a mystical celebration of the theme that is more characteristic of Whitman, not in his joyful "Songs" alone, but in his elegies as well, than any tragic consciousness, and that the note of mystical certainty and joy survived in his poetry through intermittent crises to constitute its dominant note till the very end. Thus I do not connect Whitman at all with Melville, the great tragedian of the mind. Another study of Whitman as a poet of sex and death is Clark Griffith's "Sex and Death: The Significance of Whitman's Calamus Themes," *Philological Quarterly*, XXX, No. 1 (January, 1960), 18–38. The author shows that Whitman did come to terms with abnormality and make it a part of his philosophy.

[10] See "Mutations in Whitman's Art" in *Walt Whitman—as Man, Poet, and Legend*, Gay Wilson Allen (Carbondale: Southern Illinois University Press, 1961), pp. 46–62. In his study on the evolution of Whitman, Roger Asselineau maintains that through successive revisions Whitman became "increasingly mindful of form" and revealed an "increasingly fine artistic sense," but he admits that Whitman's growing concern with artistic form, especially in his short poems, corresponded with a thinning of poetic material and inspiration. "Whitman's Style: From Mysticism to Art," in *Whitman: A Collection of Critical Essays*, Roy Harvey Pearce (ed.) (Englewood Cliffs, N.J.: Prentice-Hall, 1962), reprinted from *The Evolution of Walt Whitman*, Part II (Cambridge, Mass., 1962).

[11] Cf., "All Aquiver in a Revolt," Review of Malcolm Cowley's edition of *Leaves of Grass* (1855) by G. W. Allen, *New York Times Book Review* (February 28, 1960), p. 42. Also Richard Chase: "The Great poems of Whitman's middle period, 'Out of the Cradle,' 'As I Ebb'd,' 'When Lilacs Last in the Door Yard

stature we may consider him a major poet solely on the basis of a few of these short lyrics.

Perhaps the boldest defense of "Song of Myself" came from Malcolm Cowley, who in his Introduction to the reissue of the "Deathbed Edition" of *Whitman's Complete Verse and Prose* (1948) initiated a bold reversal of attitude. He remarked in that essay: "It has become the convention among Whitman critics to describe the Lincoln dirge, 'When Lilacs Last in the Dooryard Bloom'd,' as the summit of his achievements and the one poem to be cast into bronze or chiseled into granite if all the rest of his work were to be destroyed."[12] Mr. Cowley contended that most of Whitman's best poems were his early ones and that though Whitman wrote great poems in his later period, still the "Song of Myself" is his "miracle." There is nothing in American literature that in any way resembles "Song of Myself" except as a weak copy. Mr. Cowley has reiterated his critical position in his Introduction to the reissue of the 1855 *Poems*. Mr. Cowley's thesis is that the much misprized, misinterpreted long poem "Song of Myself" is "Whitman's greatest work, perhaps his one completely realized work and one of the greatest poems of modern times," and that the other poems of the first edition, though of an inferior order, are still examples of Whitman's freshest and boldest style. Mr. Cowley's enthusiasm for these early poems, and for "Song of Myself" especially, is inspired by his very sure insight into the inner meanings of these poems and by his appreciation of the concept of self which forms their central theme. Much of the misunderstanding of "Song of Myself," as he suggests, has been due to a wrong emphasis on its sources in contemporary American culture, whereas the poem is better understood as "one of the great inspired prophetic works that have appeared at intervals in the Western world." Mr. Cowley further suggests that "Song of Myself" is better understood when considered in relation to such great mystical writings as Christopher Smart's "Jubilate Agno," Rimbaud's "Illuminations," Blake's "Marriage of Heaven and Hell,"

---

Bloom'd,' are not an *advance* over 'Song of Myself'; they are merely *different*, in style and tone."—"'Out of the Cradle' as a Romance," in *The Presence of Walt Whitman*, p. 58. Chase even suggests that "Song of Myself" is a greater poem than "Out of the Cradle," and "in many ways more characteristic of the author," *ibid.*, p. 60.

[12] Whitman, *Complete Poetry and Prose* (Deathbed Edition; Garden City, N.Y: Garden City Books, 1954), p. 34.

or Nietzsche's "Thus Spake Zarathustra"; even more profitably, in relation to the mystical philosophies of India as expounded in the Bhagavad-Gita and the Upanishads. As Mr. Cowley himself shows, the "Song of Myself," when understood in the light of the Vedantic concept of self, is seen to possess a unity of feeling and structure, and the ideas expressed therein appear to be "bolder and more coherent than is generally supposed, and philosophically a great deal more respectable."

Of course, Mr. Cowley was not the first to discover this striking kinship in thinking and experience between Whitman and the ancient Hindu scriptures, of which he speaks at length in his Introduction. Both American and Indian readers of the *Leaves* over these one hundred years have recognized these resemblances. On reading the 1855 *Poems*, Thoreau remarked that the book was "wonderfully like the Orientals," and Emerson found in it a curious mixture of the Bhagavad-Gita and the New York *Herald*. Since then, scholars, both American and Indian, have steadily attested to these resemblances. Ananda Coomaraswamy has pointed out parallels in "Song of Myself" to Buddhist ideas.[13] Still earlier, William Norman Guthrie suggested: "Yet, in spite of every effort to be clear, he [Whitman] is steadily misunderstood by most readers for years, unless they have chanced to study the Idealist philosophers of Germany, the Mystics of Christian centuries, the Neoplatonists, or, better yet, for interpreting Emerson and Whitman, the Bhagavad Gita."[14] Recent research on Whitman, by both Indian and American students, has confirmed these affinities.[15] But the Bhagavad-Gita does not present a

[13] *Buddha and the Gospel of Buddhism* (Bombay: Asia Publishing House, 1956).

[14] *Walt Whitman: The Camden Sage* (Cincinnati: Robert Clarke Co., 1897), p. 25.

[15] The only two extensive and systematic studies of Whitman's relationship to Indian thought are Dorothy Mercer's "*Leaves of Grass* and the Bhagavad Gita: A Comparative Study" (unpublished Ph.D. diss., University of California, 1933) and my own "Whitman and Indian Thought: An Interpretation in the Light of Hindu Mysticism" (unpublished Ph.D. diss., Benares Hindu University, 1950). Dr. Mercer's work, some of which appeared in a series of articles in *Vedanta and the West*, is a comparative study of ideas which states both the agreement and the differences between Whitman's ideas and the philosophical ideas of the Gita. See Dorothy F. Mercer, "Walt Whitman on Reincarnation," IX (November-December, 1946), 180–85; "Walt Whitman on Learning and Wisdom," X (March-April, 1947), 57–59; "Walt Whitman on God and the Self," X (May-June, 1947), 80–87; "Walt Whitman on Love," X (July-August, 1947), 107-13:

unified philosophical system, for in it are currents of philosophical and religious thought which are not always united in a satisfactory synthesis. Better than the Gita for interpreting Whitman's "Song of Myself" is the Vedantic doctrine of self (*ātman-brahman*) as adumbrated in the mystical verses of the Upanishads and later developed into a system by ancient Indian logicians such as Sankara.

The absence of established evidence that Whitman had any firsthand knowledge of the Hindu books has remained a serious hurdle in Whitman research. Even Whitman's published notebooks and manuscripts do not seem to throw any light on his Indian sources. As Professor Allen has remarked, "Whether Whitman had read any Oriental literature . . . the most diligent search of scholars has not yet determined."[16] Whitman's references to India are of an altogether superficial nature, and his poem "Passage to India," which might have been the only direct evidence of his enthusiasm for India, reveals no precise knowledge about it. But then it is to be wondered how, without reading the Hindu books, Whitman came unwittingly to exhibit such marked affinities with Hindu Vedantic thought. It may be, as Mr. Cowley has suggested, that Whitman's ideas were not of literary derivation but might have been suggested to him by his own personal experiences. Romain Rolland, who also perceived these affinities, doubted the Indian origin of their inspiration; he attributed it partly to the poet's own subjective realization and partly to the predilections of his background and culture.[17]

But we must not underrate the importance of books in the making of the poet of *Leaves of Grass*. That Whitman read extensively, if not systematically, and that he passed through a long period of self-instruction before "making" his poems is clear from his preparatory reading and thought. In those years while the *Leaves* was in the making, there was considerable enthusiasm in America, particularly among New Englanders, for Hindu philosophical ideas. English and American periodicals of the time carried scraps of Vedantic material

"Walt Whitman on Karma Yoga," X (September-October 1947), 150–53; "Whitman on Raja Yoga," XI (January-February, 1948), 26–31; "Whitman on Prophecy," XI (July-August, 1948), 118–23; "Limitations in *Leaves of Grass*," XII (January-February, 1949), 21–25, (May-June, 1949), 82–87.

[16] *The Solitary Singer* (New York: MacMillan Co., 1955), p. 141.

[17] Romain Rolland, *Prophets of New India* (Almora: Advaita Ashram, 1944), p. 64.

because of the vogue the Roy literature had created.[18] Whitman, who read almost everything that came his way, could have come into contact with these ideas, though again we cannot be sure. Whitman may have assimilated Vedantic ideas indirectly through the transcendentalists, and mainly through the writings of Emerson, which surely influenced him during his formative years.

Yet Whitman's mind was open to such diverse influences and currents of thought, and his reading was so diverse that it may be an extremely hazardous task to try to find the sources for *Leaves of Grass*. As Professor Allen has put it, the book was not based on one or a dozen sources, but in it Whitman fused "hints from hundreds of books with the authentic product of his own fantasy."[19] Nor does Whitman seem to have absorbed thoroughly any single system of thought. Usually, he took only those parts of a system or book congenial to his mind or adaptable to his own pattern of thinking. Sometimes he seized on isolated words and suggestive expressions, without comprehending their inner meanings. Thus, in his poems we get numerous echoes, often faint and distant, allusions and references which it may be extremely difficult to trace. A critic interested in establishing Whitman's literary sources must guard against the danger of reading into the poems his own meanings, or claiming for them exclusive resemblances which may be traced to more than one source. No amount of painstaking analysis can ever unerringly pick out all the threads that went into the texture of *Leaves of Grass*.

Whether Whitman read the Hindu books or not is a question we must be content to leave undecided at the present stage of Whitman research. Nevertheless, a study of his poetry in the light of the Vedanta can be rewarding in itself, for it is capable of revealing new facets and meanings. It can also yield a consistent and comprehensive interpretation of a large bulk of Whitman's poetic thought. In order to get at Whitman's meanings we must read his verse as mystical verse, embodying an experience that is perfectly valid and intelligible. William James and R. M. Bucke concluded that the essential quality of Whitman's

[18] Miss Adrianne Moore, in her interesting study, *Rammohun Roy and America* (Calcutta: Brahmo Samaj Press, 1942), has shown that Rammohun Roy was the medium through which Hindu philosophy of the Advaitic (non-dualistic) Vedanta kind reached New England and how he was influential in stirring in the American mind an interest in Indian thought.

[19] *Op. cit.*, p. 172.

mind was mystical. Richard Chase's argument that mysticism is not characteristic of Whitman's poetry and that the literary critic need not be concerned with it stems from a misunderstanding. Mysticism not only constitutes the fundamental meaning of Whitman's poems, but it also determines their poetic form and symbolism. The failure to recognize this fact, can lead to distorted readings, such as Chase's own opinion that "Song of Myself" is a fine example of American humor.[20] Mysticism is the informing spirit of Whitman's poetry and is inseparable from any interpretation of its meanings. Whitman himself cautioned us, "No one will get at my verses who insists upon viewing them as a literary performance, or attempt at such performance, or as aiming mainly toward art or aestheticism."[21] Though Whitman might be underestimating his own artistic achievement, this statement should caution us against overemphasizing purely formal elements in his poetry without a due consideration of its inner meanings. The present-day trend in Whitman criticism is to explore the aesthetic character of his poetry rather than to consider it as a philosophical discourse, but, as a recent writer has observed, "We cannot afford to separate the what from the how" in Whitman's poetry, the vision from the art.[22]

James E. Miller rightly emphasizes Whitman's mysticism, and approaches the structure of his poems in the light of this under-standing.[23] His interpretation of "Song of Myself" as "inverted mysticism" is an admirable analysis because it discovers a dramatic structure in the poem, though it perhaps tends to force the poem into the arbitrary mold of a step-by-step progression in the "Mystic Way" as described by Evelyn Underhill. On the whole, Miller's critical approach, like Cowley's, is sound because it takes into proper account Whitman's meanings in evaluating his artistic performance. Whitman himself stated: "Thus my form has strictly grown from my purports and facts, and is the analogy of them." It is an investigation of these "purports and facts" that will be my primary concern in this study. I propose to show that underlying all Whitman's poetry is a consistent

[20] *Walt Whitman Reconsidered* (New York: William Sloane, 1955), p. 58.
[21] "A Backward Glance," in *Complete Poetry and Selected Prose and Letters*, edited by Emory Holloway (London: Nonesuch Press, 1938), p. 873.
[22] Sholom J. Kahn, *Walt Whitman Review*, VI, No. 1 (March, 1960), 13.
[23] *A Critical Guide to Leaves of Grass* (Chicago: University of Chicago Press, 1957).

logic, a unity of theme springing from a central identity of imaginative experience. This single dominant theme is no other than the nature of consciousness itself, or the mystic center of experience which is the self.

Mysticism, as it is understood by the Vedantist, and as it finds expression in Whitman, is a way of embracing the "other"—the objective world—in an inclusive conception of self. In other words, it is a way of finding the world in the self and as the self, thus negating the opposition of the me and the not-me. It is the power to "enter upon all, and incorporate them into himself or herself," [24] as Whitman has expressed it in a slightly different context. It is such an expansive, dynamic, and exultant conception of the self that constitutes the central element of meaning in *Leaves of Grass*. Any interpretation of Whitman must take note of the presence of this unified point of view that lends cohesion and consistency to his poetry. Though Whitman made no attempt to formulate a philosophy, his writings spring from a unity of poetic experience. The whole of his poetic effort was centered in the exploration of the nature of the self. He himself stated that the intention of *Leaves of Grass* was to "express by sharp-cut self-assertion, one's Self & also, or may be still more, to map out, to throw together for America's use, a gigantic embryo or skeleton of personality. . . ." [25] Elsewhere he makes it clear that his poems have emanated from the "dilation" and pride of his own self, ". . . this electric self out of the pride of which I utter poems." [26]

Hence our approach to Whitman's poetry should be through an analysis of its key concept, namely, the self. This concept shall be our critical instrument for investigating the fundamental meanings as well as the structural elements of Whitman's poems.

That the "I" of *Leaves of Grass* is fairly central to the poems has been generally recognized, but its exact implications and its mode of operation have not been fully appreciated. Thus, Richard Chase's critical estimate of "Song of Myself" regards the self as a successful "aesthetic or compositional device" but reaches the conclusion that the poem is a "profound and lovely comic drama of the self." [27]

[24] "Thoughts" in "By the Roadside."
[25] Letter to William D. O'Connor, January 6, 1865, Holloway, *op. cit.*, p. 950.
[26] "As I Ebb'd with the Ocean of Life," in "Sea-Drift."
[27] *Op. cit.*, p. 58.

A similar estimate claims that "He [Whitman] is a player with illusion; his center is a pun on the self; his poetry is a continual shimmering on the surfaces of concealment and revelation that is at once pathetic and comical."[28] While both these estimates justly recognize the dramatic nature of Whitman's poems, they completely mistake the spirit of the drama that the poet's self enacts as the protagonist of the action. The poems are better characterized as epic or heroic actions than as comic pieces.

The authors of *Start with the Sun*, in relating Whitman to the "cosmic" tradition, would seem to reduce Whitman's mysticism to a kind of biological or organic mysticism of the life force—a physical mysticism. Thus, comparing Lawrence and Whitman, Bernice Slote writes, "Lawrence and Whitman were bardic poets who performed in the priesthood of physical mysticism." "Physical mysticism (called mystic materialism by Aldous Huxley) assumes first that the soul and the body are one; that a spiritual realization must come through, not in rejection of, the physical world."[29] James Miller connects Whitman and Thomas to the "physical" organic tradition, in which "the nudes and the monkeys are not irrelevant." True, Whitman sings the "Body Electric" and says, "And if the body were not the soul, what is the soul?" He, like Lawrence, stresses "organic connections with the cosmos" and symbiotic union with all life. But in spite of these affinities with Lawrence and Thomas, Whitman alone seems to have a highly developed conception of selfhood. Whitman celebrates the physical because in physical experience he comes to grips with the "immaterial" core of experience; and, strangely, the ecstasy of physical sensation seems to open out to him the notion of the self, the subject of the experience who transcends the experience, being still the experiencer: "Is this then a touch? quivering me to a new identity...."[30] This elusive concept of "immateriality" Whitman presents in the only way that it can be presented, through the symbolism of the material and the concrete.

Lawrence noted that the clue to Whitman's utterance lay "in the sheer appreciation of the instant moment, life surging itself into

---

[28] Fiedler, "Images of Walt Whitman," in Milton Hindus, *op. cit.*, p. 73.
[29] Miller, Shapiro, and Slote, *op. cit.*, pp. 98, 79.
[30] "Song of Myself," 28.

utterance at its very well-head." But for him the mystery of life immanence, "the quick of the universe," is "the pulsating, carnal self, mysterious and palpable." This "pulsating, carnal self" of Lawrence is not the same as Whitman's transcendental self, the subject and experiencer, which stands both in and out of its own experience, enacting a perpetual drama. Nor is the seat of this self, wherever else it may be, in the "solar plexus"—behind the stomach—where Lawrence's carnal self is located. Lawrence's soul is the instinctual self—the self that thinks with its blood. Besides, Lawrence had no sympathy for Whitman's merging and allness. For him, the self realizes its individuality in its intense separate physicality, not in an anonymous, indiscriminate all-mergence. To him Whitman's soul was an empty concept, a state of disintegration, "an addled egg"; and the poet of the self was "the poet of the soul's last shout and shriek on the confines of death." Evidently, Lawrence had no appreciation of the transcendental aspect of Whitman's self, and so quite naturally saw Whitman's significance in the fact that he was "the first heroic seer to seize the soul by the scruff of her neck and plant her down among the potsherds."[31]

I am inclined to agree with Malcolm Cowley in his emphasis on the "Song of Myself" as representing the quintessence of Whitman, without at the same time underrating the beauty of the later lyrics. In my opinion, the joyful "celebrating" songs, songs of the "dilation and pride" of the soul, are Whitman's most characteristic and most original poems, and also his most distinctive contribution to world literature. Whitman is primarily a poet of energy. That he himself thought so becomes clear from the poem "To Soar in Freedom and in Fullness of Power," published posthumously.

> I have not so much emulated the birds that musically sing,
> I have abandon'd myself to flights, broad circles,
> The hawk, the seagull, have far more possess'd me than the canary or
>     the mocking-bird,
> I have not felt to warble and trill, however sweetly,
> I have felt to soar in freedom and in fullness of power, joy, volition.

No doubt certain phases of Whitman's poetic development registered emotional tension and conflict, a sense of tragic brooding,

[31] See Preface to *New Poems* (1919), and *Studies in Classic American Literature* (Garden City, N.Y.: Doubleday & Co., Inc., 1951).

which gives his "elegies" a depth of utterance. But, in this connection, two facts seem worth remembering. First, these tragic, emotional poems by no means comprise an appreciable bulk of Whitman's poetic output; and second, even in them the poet seems to be striving to resolve his conflicts and emerge with an integrated conception of himself. Thus, the tensions of the "Calamus" phase seem to have been resolved in the reversion to the original expansive attitude of "Song of Myself" in poems like "Starting from Paumanok" and "A Song of Joys." Professor Allen has drawn attention to an interesting fact relating to the composition of the poem "Starting from Paumanok," i.e., how the poet's later revisions on "white paper" recorded a resolution of his emotional crisis.[32] Even the lyrics "Out of the Cradle" and "When Lilacs Last in the Dooryard Bloom'd" derive their strength from the fact that they record a progress from an initial crisis to its dramatic resolution at the end.

The concept of self runs as a pervasive theme throughout Whitman's poetry. Cowley's suggestion that Whitman's notion of the self changed in the course of his career is a valuable one. Clearly, the poet's exultant vision of "Song of Myself" was temporarily clouded by the emotional turmoils of the "Calamus" period and became considerably weakened in the poems of his old age. In the old-age poems the conception of the cosmic self is modified by recurring ideas of a personal god, which accord more with Christian mysticism. In "Passage to India" the theme of spiritual dynamism is blended with symbols of god-relation. In "Prayer of Columbus" and "The Mystic Trumpeter" the dominant tone is that of god-relation, and there is a recurrence of father images. On the whole, the sentimental strain, sometimes meek and mawkish, symptomatic of the poet's decline, determines the tone of the old-age poems. After about 1868, the date of "Passage to India," Whitman's poetry seems to have lost the sustained vigor which characterized its earlier phases, and lapsed into a fitful and occasional writing, the diary-jotting of a valetudinarian.

Nevertheless, the theme of the self remains to the last a persistent theme. Whitman never stops singing of the soul, though there is now

---

[32] *Op. cit.*, pp. 221–26. Cf., Asselineau's view that the pessimism of the 1860 edition has been greatly exaggerated, and that Whitman had overcome his pessimism of 1859. *The Evolution of Walt Whitman*, Part I (Cambridge, Mass., 1960), pp. 130–31.

a softening of the animal exuberance of the 1855 edition, followed by a growing inwardness, a mellowing of nature now seeking solace in the silence of eternal being. It would not, of course, be right to say, with Cowley, that Whitman lost sight of his illumined vision of the self after 1855. Cowley's extreme enthusiasm for the First Edition, which in my opinion is fully justified, unfortunately leads him to condemn a large number of truly expansive poems contained in the later editions. The theme of the dynamic self is also pursued in such later poems as "Salut au Monde" (1856), "Crossing Brooklyn Ferry" (1856), "Song of the Open Road" (1856) "Starting from Paumanok" (1860), "A Song of Joys" (1860), "Passage to India" (1868), and in many genuinely mystical passages of "Democratic Vistas." Furthermore, I think that Cowley's rather colorful account of Whitman's "beatnik" phase, the years after 1855 and before the Civil War when, according to him, Whitman was afflicted with megalomania, and his indictment of the "bumptious" nationalism of this period are judgments based on biographical data and not justified purely in terms of the work. For nowhere in the poems of this period does this megalomania manifest itself as offensively as Cowley makes out.

In interpreting Whitman's meanings, I have dwelt on a single theme, namely, his mysticism, as offering the main key to the understanding of his poetry. The distinguishing feature of Whitman's mysticism is, to borrow a phrase from William Norman Guthrie, its "egocentric perspective." Since Whitman himself believed that the whole world is but a spectrum analysis of "my soul," and since his poems constantly enact the drama of the "soul," an investigation of this concept of the soul is of paramount interest to us. It is also this constant preoccupation with the self that distinguishes Whitman from Blake or Christopher Smart and establishes his affinity with the mysticism of the Upanishads. Both Blake and Smart were essentially Christian mystics who thought in the language of biblical symbolism. "Jubilate Agno" is a work of Christian mysticism, and though Smart sounds even more eccentric and occult than Whitman, the book voices the pathetic outpourings of a prisoner seeking solace in the thought of God. In view of this observed resemblance between Whitman's "soul" and the Vedantic concept of self, and also in view of the importance of this concept in explaining Whitman's poetry, I propose the Vedanta philosophy, the logic of the Advaita or non-dualistic school more specifically, as my instrument of critical investigation. In the same connection, I shall also examine and contrast the German dialectical doctrines (of Fichte, Schelling, and Hegel), because for several reasons I consider this aspect to be of great relevance to our study of Whitman. Whitman's enthusiasm for the German idealists is well known, and his own position in relation to their doctrines needs to be clearly defined. Moreover, as the German systems also have a fully developed doctrine of self, a comparison between them and the Vedanta in relation to Whitman will clarify many crucial points of his thought. Critics have employed the dialectic method of the Germans, often very usefully, in many modern literary studies, and even in studies of Whitman. But in my opinion Whitman's poetic method reveals fundamental differences from the method of the dialectic, and these implications must be clarified. Hence, I shall contrast Whitman's mystical intuition with the polar or dialectic imagination. My main interest is in exploring Whitman's meanings, not in establishing his literary indebtedness. When read in the light of the mystical doctrines of the Upanishads, Whitman's verse seems to gain in depth and clarity. Although such a reading will not produce an evaluation of artistic performance, I hope it will provide a surer basis for such an aesthetic judgment.

# CHAPTER TWO

# Polarity versus Intuition:
# The Nature of Consciousness

## I
### "The mere fact consciousness"

The theme of self, of relating the self to the world of experience, is central to the comprehensive intent of Whitman's poems. This self, though it is the concern of metaphysics, is not to be thought of as an abstract concept or an occult matter but should be understood as that unity of experience which is basic in all human consciousness. For the subject matter of Whitman's poetry is no other than the nature of experience itself, an intimate and vital concern with and a close attentiveness to the fact of human consciousness. Thus, Whitman's poetry records the dimensions and depths of consciousness itself more than objectifications of experience in symbol and myth. Hence, the most profitable way to approach the great bulk of Whitman's poetry is to read it as a direct dramatization of the act of consciousness rather than as a symbolization embodying that act.

This mode of expression in Whitman resulted from a consciously formulated attitude toward the problem of the art of poetry. Defining the function of the American poet, Whitman wrote in his Preface to the 1855 edition: "but folks expect of the poet to indicate more than the beauty and dignity which always attach to dumb real objects—they expect him to indicate the path between reality and their souls." Again, in the poem "As They Draw to a Close" (1871), Whitman explains the aims underlying his songs,

> To put rapport the mountains and rocks and streams,
> And the winds of the north, and the forests of oak and pine,
> With you O soul.

According to him, the "most profound theme that can occupy the mind of man . . . is doubtless involved in the query: What is the fusing explanation and tie—what the relation between the (radical, democratic) Me, the human identity of understanding, emotions, spirit, etc., on the one side, of and with the (conservative) Not Me, the whole of the material objective universe and laws, with what is behind them in time and space, on the other side?"[1] In other words, the problem that Whitman addressed himself to in his poetry is a metaphysical one, namely, the exploration of the nature of subject-object relationship, that is, the nature of self-consciousness itself. The clearest enunciation of this poetic objective is contained in a poem entitled "Beginning My Studies" (1867):

> Beginning my studies the first step pleas'd me so much,
> The mere fact consciousness, these forms, the power of motion,
> The least insect or animal, the senses, eyesight, love,
> The first step I say awed me and pleas'd me so much,
> I have hardly gone and hardly wish'd to go any further,
> But stop and loiter all the time to sing it in ecstatic songs.

There is no doubt that these lines offer us the key to a large portion of Whitman's poetry, or at least the most interesting part of it. As I will attempt to show in the course of this chapter, this "mere fact consciousness," of which Whitman sings in his ecstatic songs, not only explains the fundamental meanings of Whitman's poems, but also determines to an important degree their form and technique, and hence it is the central problem that we have to confront in any attempt to interpret Whitman.

Inasmuch as Whitman's constant preoccupation is with the self and the fact of self-consciousness, an examination of some idealistic theories of consciousness will be most appropriate. The theories most relevant, in my opinion, to this study of Whitman are, first, the post-Kantian idealistic doctrines with their systematic logic of dialecticism and, second, the Hindu Vedantic doctrine of intuition, adumbrated in the Upanishads and later developed into a system by Sankara and other ancient Indian logicians. Since the crucial issue of this study is the distinction between "dialectic" and "intuition" in relation to our interpretation of Whitman, I propose to show that the Romantic (both German and English) theories of consciousness are predominantly dialectical in their conception and that for a proper

[1] "Carlyle from American Points of View," *Complete Poetry and Selected Prose and Letters*, edited by Emory Holloway (London: Nonesuch Press, 1938), p. 786.

understanding of Whitman a theory of intuition similar to the mystical doctrine of the Upanishads will prove more profitable. For the Romantic doctrines of consciousness, despite their claim to be "transcendental," remained basically at the level of thought and presupposed the dualism that is fundamental to thought, whereas the American transcendentalists, under the influence of Neo-Platonic and Hindu ideas, conceived a mystical doctrine of intuition or unitary vision that is genuinely "transcendental" in that it is above the dualisms inherent in rational thinking. Such a belief in a mystical consciousness is at the root of Whitman's thought and can be seen operating throughout his poetry.

Whitman, like Emerson, shared in the Romantic tradition of Coleridge and the German idealists, and his concern with the problems of consciousness was part of the contemporary Romantic concern with the human mind and its operations through the creative imagination. Although Whitman never used the term "imagination" to denote consciousness—the term might have been a suspicious one to him because it carried with it the suggestion of "romance" and "fiction" which he denounced—a definite belief in intuition or "philosophic imagination" is the fundamental assumption of his thinking. Of Whitman's literary predecessors, both Coleridge and Emerson had formulated elaborate theories of imagination, variously called reason, intuition, and the like, which were at once theories of knowledge and theories of poetic creation. The basic presupposition of all Romantic doctrine was, of course, an idealistic metaphysics and a theory of perception that alloted to the human mind an active creative role in experience. The question whether the mind was a mere passive recipient of sense data, a *tabula rasa* acted upon by external stimuli, or whether it produced in any sense its own experience, was a crucial issue with the Romantics. Coleridge reacted sharply against Lockean sensationalism and the associationist psychology of Hume and Hartley and found in the idealistic thought from Plato to Kant an effective repudiation of the mechanistic theories. He derived his theory of imagination[2] from his epistemology and metaphysics, and in the

[2] For an excellent discussion of this subject, see James Volant Baker, *The Sacred River: Coleridge's Theory of Imagination* (Baton Rouge: Louisiana State University Press, 1957). Also I. A. Richards, *Coleridge on Imagination* (London: Kegan Paul, 1934).

formulation of his ideas he was guided chiefly by Plotinus and the German idealists, though he was also indebted to Spinoza, Berkeley, and Leibnitz, all of whom provided an answer to the whole school of seventeenth- and eighteenth-century mechanist psychologists. Plotinus suggested the root image of the projector, which became the favorite Romantic metaphor of the mind, and his theory of perception attributed to the conceiving mind the power of investing beauty on its material.

> This essence or character was not in the material, but it was in the conceiving mind, even before it entered into the stone. But it was in the artist not by virtue of his having eyes and hands, but by virtue of his imagination. And this beauty already comprehended in his imagination was far greater.[3]

The Plotinian figure of the soul as an overflowing fountain or a lamp radiating light replaced the mechanistic image of the mirror merely reflecting the images presented to it by the senses.[4] Besides, Plotinus had a well-defined theory of intuition according to which the soul is said to apprehend the transcendent unity of the godhead, the one, by a species of knowledge in which there is complete coalescence or identity of the knower and the known. This conception of intuition provided the basis for Coleridge's thinking, though in its final formulations his transcendental philosophy took on a dialectical cast, following the doctrines of Fichte and Schelling.

Coleridge accepted the Kantian distinction between understanding and reason, the understanding as a reflective and discursive faculty depending on the material of the senses for its exercise, and the reason as "the power of universal and necessary convictions, the source and substance of truths above sense." Kant also supplied him with the basic concept of imagination, which as an aesthetic faculty is both productive and free, and remodels and rearranges experience. But the Kantian imagination, though it is free from the laws of association, is still not a genuinely creative function, unlike Coleridge's primary imagination, for it merely synthesizes the data of the senses drawn from external nature and does not determine it in any way. Coleridge

[3] Enneads, 5.8.1. Quoted in Richards, *op. cit.*, p. 27.
[4] See M. H. Abrams, *The Mirror and the Lamp* (New York: Norton Library, 1958).

denied Kant's view that the ideas of the senses were imposed upon the consciousness rather than determined by it, and also his skeptical conclusion that absolute knowledge was denied to the human mind. It was, above all, in the philosophies of Fichte and Schelling that Coleridge found a comprehensive doctrine of consciousness and a metaphysics that accorded to the human mind a fully spontaneous and creative role.

Fichte refuted Kant's theory of unknowability and affirmed the capacity of reason to know reality. Reality is not transcendent but is itself identical with experience; otherwise knowledge would be impossible. Kant assumed dogmatically the existence of things-in-themselves, but Fichte put forward a doctrine of "idealism" according to which the object is not given but made. The thing-in-itself is thus abolished and made but a thought in the ego. Fichte conceived reality to be of the nature of self-consciousness and sought to bring out the structural principles of the knowing act. The knowing act consists in the distinction within consciousness of subject and object. Subject and object must be opposed to one another, since otherwise there could be no real consciousness. The ego or the subject posits the non-ego in order that it may become conscious of itself, and transcends this self-created opposition by a third act of consciousness, a synthesis in which the opposites are reconciled. Thus, the knowing process is the perpetual transcendence of a self-created limit. An absolute, pure subject without this self-division would, according to Fichte, be an unthinkable abstraction. Schelling, too, based his "transcendental idealism" on the structure of self-consciousness. To him, as to Fichte, consciousness is a synthetic act, a trinity or a triadic form. There is the first act of intelligence, the consciousness of self as pure activity, which gives rise to the second act, the consciousness of the not-self as a limit to that activity. The two acts are combined in the third act or the third inclusive term in which they exist simultaneously. Thus, what emerges from this logic is the concept of a triadic self, which by virtue of its inner dynamism generates its own opposition, and perpetually strives to transcend the obstacles it has thus imposed upon itself. This triadic process suggested to the Romantics yet another metaphor of the mind, which, along with the Plotinian archetype of the lamp supplied an effective answer to the mechanistic concepts.

Coleridge drew his epistemology largely from Schelling and adopted his dialectical scheme. He assumed with Fichte and Schelling that "All knowledge rests on the coincidence of an object with a subject, . . . of the thought with the thing, of the representation with the thing represented." This coincidence of subject and object is not, however, an "indifference," according to these dialecticians, but a "coalition" or union of opposites in which both the terms are present "coinstantaneously." Like Schelling, Coleridge recognized that though the self is originally the identity of object and subject, it must dissolve this identity in order to be conscious of itself, and thus it becomes an object to itself. The principle of consciousness consists in a perpetual act of self-duplication. Spirit or self can be conceived neither as subject nor as object exclusively, neither as infinite nor as finite, but "as the most original union of both." "In the existence, in the reconciling, and the recurrence of this contradiction consists the process and mystery of production and life." Coleridge's theory of imagination is also based on this dialectical framework. The aesthetic imagination, like the principle of consciousness itself, is a self-forming, self-generating act, an "esemplastic" faculty, fusing or reconciling opposites into a unity. It is a dialectical function which is motivated by an internal dynamism, an "interanimation" between its opposite poles. In the words of Coleridge himself, "that synthetic and magical power, to which I would appropriate the name of Imagination . . ." "reveals itself in the balance or reconcilement of opposite or discordant qualities: of sameness with difference, of the general with the concrete, the idea with the image, the individual with the representative. . . ." This polar tension within consciousness itself is parallelled by tension between mind on the one hand and nature on the other, and tension within nature itself. Nature, like intelligence, is self-generative, and rises through various grades up to organized and intelligent beings; and imagination is the "mediatress" that bridges the gulf between mind and matter.[5]

This dialectical method of reconciling opposites, which to Fichte and Schelling was the organ of philosophy, was further systematized by Hegel. Ratifying Fichte's criticism of Kant's assumptions, Hegel found truth to be of the nature of reason or conceptual thinking, and

[5] Coleridge, *Biographia* (London: Oxford University Press, 1958), Vol. I, chaps. xi, xii.

identified thought and reality. Consistent with this dialectic logic he found greater reality in "becoming" than in "being." Being is an empty concept; reality like thought is a unity of opposites. Dialectic, instead of annulling the opposites, unifies them by the process of self-meditation. Thus, the opposition of being and non-being is synthesized in the higher category of becoming. Dialectic, as Hegel understands it, is the consciousness of the interminable conflict in reason and the consequent attempt to resolve the conflict by rising to a higher standpoint. It depends upon recognizing that truth is a synthesis of antithetical moments, which does not ignore but unifies opposition. Concrete concept, the dialectical organ, seeks to unify opposites without annulling them. Contradictions are sought to be resolved by synthesizing them into a unity. But, in actuality, they are only avoided, not resolved,[6] as the contradictions of the lower category are included in the higher category, and those of the higher in a still higher and so on till all of them are finally enfolded and preserved in the absolute. As reality is a thought process, and as thought cannot work without opposition, opposition itself becomes, not a mere accident, but a necessary moment of the expression of reality. The absolute develops resistance; the self in order to realize its selfhood conceives itself as opposed by a not-self. Dialectic, thus, subsists on an inner differentiation. Thought refuses to dispense with differences, for the moment there is no "other," thought disappears. Accordingly, the only knowledge is that which, without negating contradictions, absorbs and unifies them in a synthesis. Truth is identity-in-difference. Simple identity or absolute non-difference is an empty concept.

This polar logic, whose essence is the spirit of opposition and transcendence (or conquest), appears as a dominant strain in Western, and particularly Romantic, thought. It goes back to Heraclitus' doctrine of the mingling of opposites: "'Men do not know,' he says, 'how what is at variance agrees with itself. It is an attunement of opposite tensions, like that of the bow and the lyre.'"[7] It appears in Bruno's principle of the synthesis of opposites, and in Jacob Boehme, who said that "without contrasts there is neither life nor manifes-

[6] P. T. Raju, *Thought and Reality: Hegelianism and Advaita* (London: George Allen, 1937), p. 80.

[7] Bertrand Russell, *A History of Western Philosophy* (New York: Simon & Schuster, 1945), p. 43.

tation. Without contrast, without another, there is only internal immobility, stillness and repose."[8] It is also seen to be the root idea of Blake's "Marriage of Heaven and Hell": "Without contraries there is no progression. Attraction and Repulsion, Reason and Energy, Love and Hate, are necessary to human existence." To Coleridge, as we have already seen, the tension between polar opposites is the central mystery of life and being. "Every power in nature and in spirit must evolve an opposite, as the sole means and condition of its manifestation: and all opposition is a tendency of reunion. . . . This identity of thesis and antithesis is the substance of all being."[9] The dialectic, no doubt, is a most powerful vehicle of a dynamic philosophy; and therefore, it is no wonder that the Romantics discovered in it the secret principle of the creative, vitalistic imagination. No wonder also that critics of our own time have been rewarded in their use of the dialectic principle. Kenneth Burke has built a whole philosophy of "dramatism" on the dialectical scheme, and modern theories of poetry as "tension" presuppose a dialectic logic. The dialectic method has also been applied to interpretations of poetic works, Burke's study of Keats's "Grecian Urn" in terms of dramatistic (or dialectical) transformation being an instance. Critics have observed a dialectical structure and development in Emerson's essays and poems,[10] and some studies of Whitman, which I shall have occasion to criticize later in the chapter, have attempted to interpret him in the light of the Hegelian dialectic. But, as I hope to demonstrate, the whole spirit and formation of Whitman's poetry is opposed to the dialectical principle. Whitman's "Song of Myself," even like Emerson's "Brahma" or Thoreau's "Walden," reveals a realm of consciousness that is fundamentally different in spirit and structure from the dialectical principle. It is the realm of mystical consciousness as it appears in the inspired utterances of the Bhagavad-Gita and the Upanishads that we should now proceed to examine; we shall make that the vantage point from which we can consistently interpret Whitman's meanings. Whitman's poetic thought operates on the principle of intuition, that is, by the method of annulling opposition, and not on the principle of the dialectic, that is, by the

[8] Quoted in James Volant Baker, *op. cit.*, p. 130.

[9] Quoted in Baker, *op. cit.*, p. 134.

[10] Richard P. Adams, "Emerson and the Organic Metaphor," in *Interpretations of American Literature*, edited by Charles Feidelson and Paul Brodtkorb (New York: Oxford University Press, 1959), p. 148.

method of "transcending" opposition or making opposition the condition of its own progress.

True knowledge is the non-dual knowledge of the real. It is a knowledge devoid of distinctions (*jñānam advayam*). While thought is a unity-in-difference, there is an inner nature in thought, "the felt unity," which is the immediate center of all mediate experience.[11] This inner nature of thought is the self which is identical with reality. Intuitive knowledge gives us access to this "original unity" of our experience. No knowledge is possible without a direct acquaintance with things. Judgment itself presupposes a non-judgmental acquaintance. The only means of contacting this unity at the base is "intellectual intuition"[12] or immediate cognition. For, thought, being dialectical by nature, cannot take us beyond differences; being mediate, it cannot reach the principle of immediacy within itself. The Upanishads teach that we possess a power more interior than intellect, by which we come into intimate contact with the real. Kant, no doubt, was convinced of the inadequacy of reason, but, by denying the possibility of a higher power, he also made the absolute inaccessible. Schelling, too, in his later treatises, tended to stress absolute identity or subject-object non-difference as the goal of philosophy, and both Fichte and Hegel attacked this as a completely empty concept. The most outstanding feature of Indian philosophy is that it asserts the possibility of a direct intercourse with the central reality by a species of intuitive identification. That there is a principle of unity involved in all our experience, which is a non-difference point of subject and object and which is basic to all such differentiation, that this unity itself is the inner nature of things, the real or *brahman*, and that we can know it in a state of pure immediacy—such, is the central doctrine of the Vedanta. This intuitive knowledge is not a special faculty with a limited use, nor a personal acquisition, nor a new emergence, but the very *prius* of all our experience. It has been there always, obscured by thought. It can be realized by divesting the mind of adventitious thought forms: the complete disappearance of thought is the intuition of the real.

Such an intuitive knowledge is, first, non-dual, being the negation of all opposition: "Where one perceives no other, hears no other,

[11] P. T. Raju, *op. cit.*, pp. 210–11.

[12] "Intellectual," because it is a knowing function, *jñāna*; "intuition," because it is immediate.

recognizes no other, there is fullness."[13] Intuition is pure subjectivity:

> For, where there is duality as it were, there one smells another, there one sees another, there one hears another, there one speaks to another, there one thinks of another, there one understands another. Where, verily, everything has become the self, then by what and whom should one smell, then by what and whom should one see ... by what, should one know that by which all this is known? By what, my dear, should one know the knower?[14]

Again, "Verily, that Imperishable, O Gorgi, is unseen, but is the seer, is unheard but is the hearer, unthought but is the thinker, unknown but is the knower."[15] Intuitive experience is a form of mergence, a dissolution of the "other" sense in pure consciousness. This state of pure being is described in the Upanishad by an analogy:

> As a lump of salt thrown in water becomes dissolved in water and there would not be any of it to seize forth as it were, but wherever one may take it is salty indeed, so, verily, this great being, infinite, limitless, consists of nothing but knowledge.[16]

Intuition is knowing by being. It arises by an intimate fusion of the knower and the known. It is said in the Upanishad, "the knower of Brahman becomes Brahman." Conversely, it may be said, we can know *brahman* only by being *brahman*, because real, immediate knowledge is gained by being. Being is knowing. Real knowing or absolute knowledge is immediacy, *aparōkṣa*. The knowledge which is non-dual and immediate will necessarily be one in which subject and object become one, where essence and existence, knowledge and the real coincide. Intuition is knowledge by identity. In that state of immediacy the object is merged in the subject, so that the subject is all. The knower, known, and the act of knowing are one. Thus, in intuition all dualities are dissolved.

And lastly, intuition is integral knowing. The vision it gives is the vision of the whole, a unified, synoptic vision of reality, in which the inner and the outer, the one and the many, the individual and the universal, are perceived as one. Such is the conception of consciousness

[13] Chhandogya Upanishad, 7.24.1, "*yatra nānyat paśyati, nānyat śṛṇōti, nānyat vijānāti sa bhūmā.*"
[14] Brihadaranyaka Upanishad, 2.4.14.
[15] *Ibid.*, 3.8.11.
[16] *Ibid.*, 2.4.12; Chhandogya, 6.13.2.

that is developed in the mystical verses of the Upanishads. This consciousness, which is the principle of self within all (*atman-brahman*) is, however, an ineffable experience, beyond logic and beyond speech. Hence, the Upanishadic verses give but an indirect intimation of it, negatively, in the language of paradox and through analogy, by describing what that experience may be like.

## II

It is certain that Whitman, as well as Emerson, believed in some form of intuition as the real source of knowledge. Emerson, who had a first-hand knowledge of Hindu and Neo-Platonic doctrines, accepted their insistence on intuitive knowledge. The notion of intuitive identity and spiritual oneness of being impressed him so much that it became the most important theme of his writings and the keynote to his philosophy. Whitman recognized a form of knowledge which is supersensuous and superrational, for the knowledge to be gained is of unity, not of difference, whereas both reason and the senses work on difference. To apprehend a reality that is unknowable by the intellect, and to realize the unity and harmony at the root of things, a form of cognition is required which is at once unitive and immediate. Whitman says, "from the eyesight proceeds another eyesight, and from the hearing proceeds another hearing, and from the voice proceeds another voice, eternally curious of the harmony of things with man."[17] The following is an even more explicit statement:

> There is, apart from mere intellect, in the make-up of every superior human identity . . . a wondrous something that realizes without argument, . . . an intuition of the absolute balance, . . . of the whole of this multifarious, mad chaos of fraud, . . . we call *the world*; a soul-sight of that divine clue and unseen thread which holds the whole congeries of things. . . . Such soul-sight and root-center for the mind. . . .[18]

The idea that there is a power in the constitution of every man above the intellect which gives a direct insight into the harmony underlying

[17] Preface, 1855 Edition, Holloway, *op. cit.*, p. 576.
[18] "Carlyle from American Points of View," Holloway, *op. cit.*, p. 785. Also, "There is in the soul an instinctive test of the sense and actuality of anything . . . this instinct of the soul—this self-settling power. . . ." *Complete Writings of Walt Whitman* (New York: G. P. Putnam's Sons, 1902), Vol. VI, Part I, No. 65.

the multifarious show of the world, the unity beneath the multiplicity, and that this power is a perception by the soul, and as such the root center or the foundation of our minds, is typically Vedantic. The Gita speaks of a supernatural eye, or *divya chakṣu*.[19] The Upanishad says: "Hearing they hear not; knowing they know not; seeing they see not; only with the eye of enlightenment do they see" (*paśyanti jñāna chakṣuṣā*). In his essay on "Self-Reliance," inquiring into the reason for self-trust, Emerson asks:

> What is the Trustee? What is the aboriginal Self on which a universal reliance may be grounded? What is the nature and power of that science-baffling star, without parallax, without calculable elements, which shoots a ray of beauty even into trivial and impure actions, if the least mark of independence appear? The inquiry leads us to that source, at once the essence of genius, of virtue, and of life, which we call Spontaneity or Instinct. We denote this primary wisdom as Intuition, whilst all later teachings are tuitions. In that deep force, the last fact behind which analysis cannot go, all things find their common origin. For, the sense of being which in calm hours rises, we know not how, in the soul, is not diverse from things, from space, from light, from time, from man, but one with them and proceeds obviously from the same source whence their life and being also proceed.

In his essay on "Intellect" Emerson develops the concept of an intuitive principle, which he calls "the intellect receptive," which is prior to and presupposed in all mental activity or thought construction, and which is "a union with the things known." Intellect is also integral knowing. Whereas thought works a division between man and nature, causing an internal fissure, and fastens attention on single aspects, the intellect gives an integral vision of the whole. "We live in succession, in division, in parts, in particles. . . . we see the world piece by piece, as the sun, the moon, the animal, the tree,"[20] while the whole lies hidden from our view. In "Compensation" Emerson says: "While the world will be whole and refuses to be disparted, we seek to act partially, to sunder, to appropriate." The Upanishads aver:

> This Self has entered into the bodies upto the tip of the nails . . . People do not see it, for viewed in its aspects it is incomplete. . . . When it does the function of living, it is called the vital force; when it speaks, the organ

[19] Bhagavad-Gita, 11.8.
[20] "The Over-soul."

of speech; when it sees, the eye; when it hears, the ear; and when it thinks, the mind. These are merely its names according to its functions. He who meditates upon each of this totality of aspects does not know, for it is incomplete, being divided from this totality. The Self is to be meditated upon for in it all these become one.[21]

In the essay on "Plato" Emerson expresses the spiritual identity of being and quotes from the Hindu scriptures:

"The same, the same: friend and foe are of one stuff; the ploughman, the plough and the furrow are of one stuff. . . . Men contemplate distinctions, because they are stupefied with ignorance. . . . The knowledge that this spirit, which is essentially one, is in one's own and in all other bodies, is the wisdom of one who knows the unit of things."

He affirms over and over again that subject and object are identical, that both have sprung from a common substratum of spirit: "the act of seeing and the thing seen, the seer and the spectacle, the subject and the object are one."[22]

It is Whitman's profoundest conviction that the source of wisdom is the soul, that truth wells up from a region far deeper than either the senses or the intellect. To cite only two of his typical mystical experiences: "Swiftly arose and spread around me the peace and knowledge that pass all the argument of the earth, / And I know the hand of God is the promise of my own, . . ."[23] and "When the subtle air, the impalpable, the sense that words and reason hold not, surround us and pervade us, / Then I am charged with untold and untellable wisdom, I am silent, I require nothing further."[24] The profoundest experiences of the spirit are incomprehensible and baffling to the intellect. In the Kena Upanishad we find: "The eye does not go there, nor speech, nor mind; we do not know that, we do not know how to instruct one about it. It is distinct from the known and above the unknown."[25] But though experience transcends thought, it still remains an experience. Though "untellable" it is a certainty, "Distinct from the known and above the unknown." It is not known in the sense that it is not something external; it is different from the known

[21] Brihadaranyaka, 1.4.7.
[22] "The Over-soul."
[23] "Song of Myself," 5.
[24] "Of the Terrible Doubt of Appearances," in "Calamus."
[25] Kena Upanishad, 1.3.

in the sense that it cannot be known in the way of thought, i.e., as an object. It is unknowable (*avēdya*), yet immediate (*aparōkṣa*). As Emerson puts it: "We know the truth when we see it . . . as we know when we are awake that we are awake."[26] Truth is self-proven (*svasiddha*) and self-evident. It is perceived immediately by the soul. Whitman affirms:

> Here is the test of wisdom,
> Wisdom is not finally tested in schools,
> Wisdom cannot be pass'd from one having it to another not having it,
> Wisdom is of the soul, is not susceptible of proof, is its own proof,
> Applies to all stages and objects and qualities and is content,
> Is the certainty of the reality and immortality of things and the excel-
> lence of things. . . .[27]

"Wisdom is of the soul," "is the efflux of the soul." It is something immediate and nearest to one's self, a realization of the self, by the self, in the self (*ātmānam ātmanā ātmani*).

As we see from his writings, Whitman realizes the oneness of the universe and rises to the conception of an absolute being or substance, which is at once the support and essence of the world: "Ethereal, pervading all . . . / Essence of forms, life of the real identities, perman-ent, positive (namely the unseen). . . ."[28] The thought of the oversoul as the substratum of the universe is common to Emerson and Whitman. For Whitman this oversoul is no other than one's own self.

> And lo to the consciousness of the soul, the permanent identity, the thought, the something. . . . That something is the All, and the idea of the All, with the accompanying idea of eternity, and of itself, the soul, buoyant, indestructible, sailing space forever, visiting every region, as a ship the sea. . . . And lo the Pulsation in all matter, all spirit throbbing forever—the eternal beats, eternal systole and diastole of life in things. . . .[29]

Here is the thought of the soul or "Kosmic Spirit"—permanent and indestructible, pulsating in all things and vitalizing them. The idea

---

[26] "The Over-soul." Also *Complete Writings*, Vol. VI, Part I, No. 69, "that unspeakable something in my own soul which makes me know without being able to tell how it is that I know. The greatest of thoughts and truths . . . are not susceptible of proof."
[27] "Song of the Open Road," 6.
[28] "Chanting the Square Deific," 4, in "Whispers of Heavenly Death."
[29] "Democratic Vistas," in Holloway, *op. cit.*, p. 716.

of an immutable essence, the original unity at the base of the shifting shows and materials is expressed in the following:

> Metaphysics is that which considers the whole concrete show of things, the world, man himself, either individually or aggregated in history, as resting on a spiritual invisible basis, eternally shifting, yet real substance, and the only immutable one.
>
> Penetrating beneath the shows and materials of the objective world we find, according to Hegel, (though the thought by itself is not new but very antique and Indian and Grecian) that in respect to human cognition of them, all and several are pervaded by the only absolute substance which is spirit.[30]

Emerson also expresses the same idea in "Compensation": "Under all this running sea of circumstance . . . lies the aboriginal abyss of real Being."

Whitman defines his notion of prudence in terms of a unitive, integrated vision of the whole that does not dwell on single aspects and operate by dividing and detaching one from the other.

> The prudence of the greatest poet answers at last the craving and glut of the soul, puts off nothing, permits no let up for its own case or any case, has no particular sabbath or judgement day, divides not the living from the dead, or the righteous from the unrighteous, is satisfied with the present, matches every thought or act by its correlative, and knows no possible forgiveness or deputed atonement.[31]

Prudence is a non-dual vision; it is the faculty of viewing things integrally as an all, a *sarvam*, or a whole. The Upanishad says, "He sees objects coalescing in identity (*dharmān samatām gatān paśyati*); only by delusion is the One divided (*mayayā bhidyatē he ētat*)." Similarly, Whitman's concept of the "ensemble" is to be interpreted as a unitive conception which contemplates the "perfect sense of the oneness of nature,"[32] for he says, "All must have a reference to the ensemble of the world, and the compact truth of the world, / There shall be no object too pronounced—all works shall illustrate the divine law of indirections."[33] Again, "I will not make poems with reference to parts, / But I will make poems, songs, thoughts, with

[30] *Complete Writings*, Vol. VI, Part II, No. 175.

[31] Preface, 1855, Holloway, *op. cit.*, p. 583. Also "Song of Prudence," in "Autumn Rivulets."

[32] *Ibid.*, p. 582.

[33] "Laws for Creations," in "Autumn Rivulets."

reference to ensemble." [34] Whitman's statement that "all must have a reference to the ensemble of the world" might at first appear to be Hegelian. [35] For, according to Hegel, since the universe is a "compact" system, the individual parts are not self-subsistent, each part being considered only in relation to the total scheme. Truth, on this view, would consist "in the just relation of objects to each other and to the whole." On this formula, Whitman's statement would mean that no part of the world is complete in its isolation and that for the understanding of its truth it must be considered only in reference to the totality. This same meaning could be found in Emerson's statement, "While the world will be whole and refuses to be disparted." But, considering the high regard in which both Emerson and Whitman hold the individual person or object, and the unique status they accord to it, we should understand the above passages rather as cases of a unitive, non-dualistic vision than as illustrations of the Hegelian logic. In the context of their individualism the statements might be interpreted to mean that the world is a unity, an undifferentiated whole, as distinct from the Hegelian whole differentiated into the totality of its parts, and that as a result of the "dividing and detaching" habit of the mind things are seen as different and multiple while in fact they are one. Both Emerson and Whitman reiterate over and over that each individual aspect is in itself the whole of reality and expresses its fullest meaning; this convicion is, in fact, the central point of their philosophies. Such passages in Emerson as: "Yet does the world reappear in miniature in every event," "the world globes itself into a drop of dew," "God reappears with all his parts in every moss and cobweb," illustrate this viewpoint. Whitman's all-embracing vision of "omnes" and "en masse," while it transcends all limited forms and particularity, praises the absolute worth and reality of every existent fact and sees "a world in a grain of sand." "He that perceives the nature of a single one perceives the nature of all." [36]

Dr. Bucke has shown that Whitman may be regarded as the greatest instance of "cosmic consciousness," for in Whitman one can find the cosmic sense fully developed. [37] Cosmic consciousness, which is

[34] "Starting from Paumanok," 12.

[35] For a complete treatment of Whitman and Hegel, see chap. vi below.

[36] See Sankara's commentary on Chhandogya, 6.4.4.

[37] *Cosmic Consciousness* (14th ed.; New York: E. P. Dutton & Co., Inc., 1948).

the same as the intuitional sense, enables man to realize the oneness of the universe. To Whitman this intuitional sense is no other than the principle of self involved in consciousness. The principle of self, with its tremendous sweep, overreaches all obstacles and embraces the whole within itself. Cosmic consciousness is the consciousness of the self that is the cosmos, the one that is the all, the *atman*, the internal principle which is also the mighty universal Brahman. This intuitional sense operates, first, by dissolving opposition and not by setting up opposition, and thus it establishes subject-object identity. This dissolving activity of the intuition is best affirmed in the paradoxical expression. Second, it gives an expansive cosmic vision and releases an inner dynamism of spirit, which causes the mind to experience sensations such as inclusiveness, penetration and depth, and fluidity and motion. The concepts of space and time, astronomical expanses, sea and river images and the like are seen to be the appropriate symbols of this intuitional sense. It will be the purpose of the succeeding section to follow the operations of this intuitional act in the form and symbolism of some of Whitman's poetry.

## III

fluid and swallowing soul"
("Song of Myself," 33)

Whitman's poems of "self" may be read as a dramatization or enactment of the intuitive activity. Whitman conceives of the role of the poet as a "joiner," "as blender, uniter," who tightly holds the hands of nature and soul. "Which he will never release until he reconciles the two, / And wholly and joyfully blends them."[38] The central issue of Whitman's poetry, then, is finding an answer to the question, "What is the fusing tie between the soul and the world, the subject and the object, mind and matter?" or the question of the nature of consciousness itself. The classic statement of this problem is expressed in the form of a paradox, which is a major stylistic device in Whitman's verse. "One's-self I sing, a simple separate person, / Yet utter the word Democratic, the word En-Masse."[39] The first line asserts the individual being's uniqueness of identity. The second presents the seemingly opposite concept of the aggregate. The purport of the whole is to

[38] "When the Full-grown Poet Came," in "Good-Bye My Fancy."
[39] In "Inscriptions."

affirm the identity of the two.[40] In another statement of this type he says, "Strange and hard the paradox true I give, / Objects gross and the unseen soul are one."[41] Yet this state of identity is not achieved through any visible process; there is no bridge, no middle category connecting the me and the not-me. The one does not become the other through any process of mediation, and it cannot, in fact, "become" the other without losing its identity. The individual which becomes the other or posits the other as a condition of its own exist- ence ceases to be individual, that is, unique and indivisible. Here is a logical impasse. Evidently, dialectic cannot solve it. There must, there- fore, be a sense, immediate and self-proven, in which both the cate- gories of self and not-self are given as being one. But this oneness, being beyond logic and language, can be stated only in paradoxical form,[42] as "it is and is not." The characteristic form of the mystical utterances in the Upanishads is the paradox: "To whomsoever it is not known, to him it is known, to whomsoever it is known, to him it is not known. Unknown to those who know, and known to those who do not know."[43] The paradoxical form is the only way in which the in- tuition of the unitary self can be affirmed. The heart of the paradox as a form of language affirmation is the denial of dualities. Hence, Whitman *assumes* that his own self is the self of all; he celebrates himself, and, *therefore*, celebrates "you." It can be seen that the poet effects the transition from the self to the "other" by an "intuitive leap." Contemplating a shroud, the poet becomes the shroud and dramatizes its being: "A shroud I see and I am a shroud, I wrap a body and lie in the coffin."[44] Again, "I am a dance—play up there!"[45] And at another point, "Distant and dead resuscitate, / They show as the

[40] Contrast Kenneth Burke's interpretation of these lines: "No two opening lines of a poet's work ever indicated more clearly the sheer dialectics of a position. . . ." See "Policy Made Personal," in Milton Hindus, *Leaves of Grass One Hundred Years After* (Stanford, Calif.: Stanford University Press, 1955), p. 82.

[41] "A Song for Occupations," 5.

[42] "The assertions of faith are one and all paradoxes." Quoted in Ben F. Kempel, *Language and Religion* (New York: Philosophical Library, 1957), p. 94; see also Bertrand Russell, *Mysticism and Logic* (New York: Longmans, Green & Co., 1918). The mystic's belief in unity and his refusal to admit opposition or divi- sion anywhere appears in the simultaneous assertion of contradictory propositions.

[43] Kena, 2.3.

[44] "The Sleepers," 2.

[45] *Ibid.*, 1.

dial or move as the hands of me, I am the clock myself."[46] In the last of these quotations, it is interesting to study the transitions through which the objects, "distant and dead" are metaphorically transformed into the dial, and then into "the hands of me," into the self, the last part, "I am the clock myself" being but a logical extension of that metaphor. This intuitive transposition of the subject is effected in a flash, as if by a mere change of slide, as when the poet, speaking of the buds, "Do you not know ... how the buds beneath are unfolded," suddenly identifies himself with the bud, "leaps" into her being by an invisible transition:

> Waiting in gloom protected by frost,
> The dirt receding before my prophetical screams,
> I underlying causes to balance them at last.[47]

Sometimes, the transition from the object to the subject is marked by just four periods:

> Now the vast bulk that is the whale's bulk ... it seems mine,
> Warily, sportsman! though I lie so sleepy and sluggish,
> My tap is death.[48]

Also in the following lines the leap from the object to the subject is quick and dramatic. The poet is describing the beauty of a gigantic stallion: "His nostrils dilate as my heels embrace him, / His well-built limbs tremble with pleasure as we race around and return."[49]

The poem "There Was a Child Went Forth" offers us the key to the workings of Whitman's poetic mind. The efficacy of the intuitive mind is such that it annihilates all illusory mental barriers that seem to separate the self from the world of objects. The object which to the senses and the thinking mind appears as an obstacle to be overcome "flows and unites" and merges with the subject.

> There was a child went forth every day,
> And the first object he look'd upon, that object he became,
> And that object became part of him for the day or a certain
>     part of the day,
> Or for many years or stretching cycles of years.
> . . . . . . . . . . . . . . . . . . . . . . . . . . . . . . . . . . .

[46] "Song of Myself," 33.
[47] *Ibid.*, 25.
[48] "The Sleepers," 6 (1855 edition).
[49] "Song of Myself," 32.

These became part of that child who went forth every day
and who now goes, and will always go forth every day.

Similarly, the symbolism of the poem, "The Sleepers," is centered in the theme of intuitive identification. This poem, like "Song of Myself," owes its dramatic quality to the activities of the intuitional self performing its cosmic drama of identification. "I dream in my dream all the dreams of the other dreamers, / And I become the other dreamers." The central "motif" of the poem is, of course, the self that wanders "all night in my vision" both as a spectator and a participant, assuming the myriad roles of "the actor and the actress . . . the voter . . . the politician." Night and sleep, which on the physical level join the "antipodes" and unite all separate-seeming entities into an undifferentiated mass, stand as symbolic equivalents of the unifying activity of the intuitive vision. Like the self itself which pervades and enfolds the "multiverse" of objects, "The night pervades them and enfolds them." In "Our Old Feuillage" the "American soul," which is no other than the poet's self, sweeps the expansive scene of the New World horizon:

Encircling all, vast-darting up and wide, the American Soul, with equal
    hemispheres, One Love, one Dilation or Pride;

The soul matches the wide "outer" horizon with its own "inner" ("equal") hemispheres, one of love and the other of dilation. Then it "becomes" all the lands and scenes and sets out on a free flight "into" them all:

O lands! all so dear to me—what you are, (whatever it is,) I putting it
    at random in these songs, become a part of that, whatever it is,
Southward there, I screaming, with wings slow flapping, with the
    myriads of gulls wintering along the coasts of Florida,
. . . . . . . . I with the spring waters laughing and skipping and running,
. . . . . . . . I with parties of snowy herons . . .
. . . . . . . . and I triumphantly twittering. . . . . . . .
        .       .       .       .       .       .       .       .
Cities, labors, death, animals, products, war, good and evil—these me. . .

"Chanting the Square Deific" ("Whispers of Heavenly Death") affords another example of the poet's cosmic expansion. Advancing out of the One (Godhead), the poet vicariously identifies himself in turn with each side of the Divine Square dramatizing its fourfold character of justice, benevolence, evil (or the spirit of disobedience and revolt), and Santa Spirita. The poet's soul is the "general soul" or the Oversoul, the center and essence of the universe.

It is by such intuitive leaps that the poet enacts the drama of identification. Like some mercurial substance, the self penetrates into the heart of all being, "backward as well as forward sluing, / To niches aside and junior bending."[50] The intuitive vision rends the veil of *maya* and penetrates into the core of the object, for the true nature of the object is its interiority. So Whitman asks:

> Only the kernel of every object nourishes;
> Where is he who tears off the husks for you and me?
> Where is he who undoes stratagems and envelopes for you and me?[51]

Hence, "The poets of the cosmos advance through all interpositions and coverings and turmoils and strategems to first principles."[52] True insight, in the words of Emerson, "pierces the form, overleaps the wall" and penetrates the material husk of reality to its core. "With each divine impulse the mind rends the thin rinds of the visible and finite, and comes out into eternity, and inspires and expires its air."[53] To Thoreau this intuitive faculty is "a cleaver," "it discerns and rifts its way into the secret of things"; "it is an organ for burrowing."[54] Whitman calls this intuitional sense the "fluid and swallowing soul."

> I fly those flights of a fluid and swallowing soul,
> My course runs below the soundings of plummets.
>
> .    .    .    .    .    .    .    .    .
>
> You light surfaces only, I force surfaces and depths also.[55]

This experience of depth and fluidity, of "concentration" and expansion, is characteristic of the intuitional sense. The intuitional mind "sees into the life of things" and embraces the infinite in one sweep. Whitman calls this the "Eye to pierce the deepest deeps and sweep the world."[56] The activity of this mind is intimated in the following passage: "Great is the faith of the flush of knowledge, and of the investigation of the depths of qualities and things. Cleaving and

[50] *Ibid.*, 13.
[51] "Song of the Open Road," 6.
[52] Preface, 1855, Holloway, *op. cit.*, p. 581.
[53] "The Over-soul."
[54] *Walden*, chap. xi.
[55] "Song of Myself," 33, 40.
[56] "By Blue Ontario's Shore," 9.

circling here swells the soul of the poet, yet is president of itself always. The depths are fathomless, and therefore calm."[57]

The operations of the intuitional mind can be seen through all of Whitman's expansive poems of the self. The "fluid and swallowing soul" manifests itself symbolically in the alternation of kinetic and "depth" images, and through dynamic symbols like space, time, and sea, and through a perpetual motion in both outward and inward directions. But, of these symbolic voyages of the soul, and of the nature of Whitman's dynamism, I shall have occasion to speak later on. With the abolition of the subject-object barriers the mind attains great elasticity and expresses itself in dynamic expansion. In "Song of Myself" is expressed this exalted sense of mystical self-expansion, which is the highest achievement of the intuitional sense. In it is also seen the way in which the poet negotiates with the world of objects, not through the dialectical process of setting up oppositions and transcending them but by intuitive identification. The following lines should suffice to bring out the force of our argument.

> The disdain and calmness of martyrs,
> The mother of old, condemn'd for a witch, burnt with dry wood,
> > her children gazing on,
> The hounded slave that flags in the race, leans by the fence,
> > blowing, cover'd with sweat,
> The twinges that sting like needles his legs and neck,
> > the murderous buckshot and the bullets,
> All these I feel or am.
>
> I am the hounded slave, I wince at the bite of the dogs,
> .   .   .   .   .   .   .   .   .   .
> I do not ask the wounded person how he feels,
> > I myself become the wounded person.[58]

Thus, the poet's mind runs through the whole gamut of life and death, vicariously participating in the cosmic life. In this sublime vision of expansion the soul, freed of its impediments, becomes perfectly fluid and diaphanous and reflects the cosmic existence within itself. Quicksilver-like it flows through all things and swallows their meanings. Intuition is that faculty which gives a sense of *sarvātmatva*, at-oneness with the all. In it the soul expands to the universal.

[57] Preface, 1855, Holloway, *op. cit.*, p. 579.
[58] "Song of Myself," 33.

The perception which breaks through subject-object barriers and melts down all solid-seeming things into an "eternal float of solution" must also be one which reduces the congealing categories of time and space into a vast spiritual continuum. "Crossing Brooklyn Ferry" presents in a most beautiful form this intuitive transcendence of space and time. Not only is the poem rich in symbol and imagery, it is perhaps Whitman's most successful treatment of the theme of consciousness in terms of the "spatial form." The fact of consciousness, subsisting in the moment and not in "duration," can be presented only spatially, that is, as discrete images representing moments of consciousness, and not as a temporal sequence. It can be apprehended only spatially in an instant of time, that is to say, in space and not as a series of temporal repetitions. Paradoxically enough, the flow of time itself is grasped as a frozen, concrete shape, and motion grasped as a motionless condition in a moment of time. It is the presentation of this "spatialized" consciousness that gives "Crossing Brooklyn Ferry" its deep symbolic meaning and its rich paradoxical implication. The ride across the river, the flow of the water, and the flow of time suggested by the physical motion are realized in a unified spatial apprehension, "motionless in a moment of time." "The current rushing so swiftly and swimming with me far away" sets the poet's mind in motion by suggesting a spiritual continuum in which all things flow and fuse into one another and stand suspended in an "eternal float of solution." The sense of far and near, and of past, present, and future are merged in the consciousness of the eternal moment. "The float for ever held in solution" or the continuum suggested by the flowing river and the motion of the ferry enables the poet to establish meditative communion with future generations crossing the river: "It avails not, time or space—distance avails not, / I am with you, you men and women of a generation, or ever so many generations hence." In this intuitive mergence the world of the present and the future exist simultaneously in a unified perceptual apprehension in a moment of vision. Yet, curiously enough, all this flow and motion suggested in the poem takes place only against the fixed, unchanging background of nature, the "mast-hemm'd Manhattan" and the sights on its shore, and on the higher level, the eternally enduring fact of consciousness itself. Thus, the poem achieves the paradoxical result of suggesting through movement the suspension of movement, of grasping time-flow in a sensation that involves the halting of time-flow. The total meaning of the poem is the suggestion of a realm of experience that is beyond time and space, arrested in a single intuitive act. And this meaning, as I have noted here, is achieved paradoxically by "flow" symbols that suggest the suspension of flow. Thus, the opening lines of stanza 9 begin with an invocation to the river to flow on to aid the flow of time and life, but in the eighth line of the stanza the poet asks the eternal flow to stand suspended. "Suspend here and everywhere, eternal float of solution!"[59]

This suggestion of fixity in motion is in the basic symbolism of the poem; but it is made even more explicit in a few images which, though of a secondary order, still seem to have a bearing on the function of the primary symbols in the poem, if they are not interpreted too literally.

> Just as you stand and lean on the rail, yet hurry with the swift current,
> *I stood yet was hurried* ....
>
> . . . sea-gulls, saw them high in the air *floating with motionless wings.* . . .
>
> Be firm, rail over the river, to support those who lean idly, *yet haste with the hasting current.* . . . (Italics mine.)

This paradoxical juxtaposition of motion and fixity has the effect of arresting all motion in a fixed moment of experience; it gives us a direct insight into the nature of consciousness itself, as consisting in the moment, in eternal being, not in time or in Bergsonian *durée* which, like a musical structure, is an accumulation of the ever surging flow of time.

In his Preface to the 1855 edition Whitman conceives of the role of the poet as a "time-binder"[60] who competes with the laws of time and brings the spirit of all events and scenes to bear on the mind of the reader "in an instant of time." "Past, present and future are not disjoin'd but join'd," and the poet "places himself where the future becomes present." The implication of this doctrine of time is that all time process is grasped and presented as crystallized into an instant,

---

[59] Here the correct interpretation of the word "suspend" would seem to be, "stand suspended," meaning a condition of being suspended in flow or motion, with its paradoxical implication. For an alternative meaning see Gay Wilson Allen and Charles T. Davis, *Walt Whitman's Poems* (New York: New York University Press, 1955), critical note on the poem, p. 158.

[60] I borrow this phrase from Allen and Davis, *op. cit.*, p. 9.

and not as a succession. This theory might at first resemble Bergson's concept of *duration* and Croce's concept of *historie*. But in its true implication it is opposed to Bergson's doctrine. Whitman does not conceive of time in Bergsonian terms as "the continuous progress of the past which gnaws into the future," as an ever surging current which swells with the "duration" it accumulates. Nor does Whitman subscribe to Bergson's view of mind itself as a *durée*. In opposition to Bergson, Whitman definitely assumes the existence of an unchanging "ego" which runs through all changing states of experience, like a string through the beads of a necklace.[61] Whitman's is not a time philosophy,[62] but a time-negating philosophy. When Whitman speaks of his function as "time-binding," he implies "time-abolishing."

Since Whitman's purpose is the explication of consciousness as consisting in the eternal moment, he presents it spatially in terms of a succession of visual patterns, not as a temporal structure. In this "spatial" presentation of events, each or any single event is a self-complete monad containing the whole of consciousness. A large bulk of Whitman's poetry builds on this visual principle and presents endless successions of images or events containing moments of realized vision. It is remarkable that none of Whitman's more important poems, except the elegiac poems like "Lilacs" and "Out of the Cradle," presents a dramatic transformation, dialectical or otherwise, such as Kenneth Burke has discovered in Keat's "Grecian Urn," or builds a narrative structure. The fact of the matter is that Whitman's poetry is concerned not with the transformation of events in time but with the fact of consciousness itself as captured in an instant. Whitman's form, as he himself asserted, "has strictly grown from my purports and facts, and is the analogy of them," [63] and as such is suited for the presentation of consciousness as a spatial form. Critics have observed that one of the most distinctive features of Whitman's poetic style is that it is built on the self-contained line as the basic unit.[64] The secret of Whitman's style is this "flash of revelation in

[61] *sutrē maṇigaṇā iva.*

[62] See Wyndham Lewis, *Time and Western Man* (New York: Harcourt, Brace & Co., 1928), and C. E. M. Joad, *Introduction to Modern Philosophy* (Oxford: Clarendon Press, 1925), on Bergson.

[63] Preface to Centennial Edition, Holloway, *op. cit.*, p. 735.

[64] See S. Musgrove, *T. S. Eliot and Walt Whitman* (Wellington: New Zealand University Press, 1952), p. 25.

the individual phrase and word."[65] The lines progress by accumu-
lating images which succeed each other following no logic except that
they appear in free association. Each of these images is a self-sufficient
universe, and hence does not function in a dramatic context, being itself
the dramatic focus. Eliot's images, on the other hand, are highly
functional, for they contribute to the general structure of meaning,
as in the line from "Gerontion": "The goat coughs at night in the
field overhead." Our impatience with Whitman's catalogues, justified
perhaps, is born of our failure to pause and dwell with the poet on the
ecstasy of every single sensation. Our mind functions by selecting and
ordering and searches for conclusiveness and dramatic development.
It is just these elements that Whitman's enumerations seem to lack.
Whitman exults in the perfect miraculousness of every object, of every
existent fact, and infuses himself into all being. He peruses "manifold
objects, no two alike, and every one good, . . . / Every kind for itself
and its own"[66] Though more often Whitman is content with mere
enumerations, he can employ his catalogues for a more dramatic
purpose. Sometimes, the catalogues move with a cumulative force,
gathering strength as they go toward a dramatic affirmation. Thus, in
Section 4 of "Song of Myself," after listing the things and men and
events that surround him, he confronts us with the sudden brief
affirmation: "But they are not the Me myself." Coming after the long
catalogue of things this line strikes us with a direct impact. Again, in
Sections 8, 15, and 33 the poet follows up an interminable list of things
and men and their doings with dramatic and conclusive utterances:
"I mind them or the show or the resonance of them—I come and I
depart." "These one and all tend inward to me, and I tend outward
to them," and "I tread day and night such roads." The images in
Whitman following in long processions, while they individually
function as self-complete units of meaning, also produce a cumulative
effect of telescoping a vast stretch of experience into a mosaic of visual
pattern. Thus, in "Salut au Monde," which is in Whitman's most
characteristic style, the poet's expansive vision is presented in terms of
these image processions. These images, however, do not terminate
in mere sensation but constantly point to the experiencing subject,
the "I" as the active, unifying principle. Though the vision is of the

[65] Milton Hindus, *op. cit.*, p. 9.
[66] "Song of Myself," 7.

ever shifting sights and sounds seen and heard, the subject itself runs through all the successions, constant and unchanged. "What cities the light or warmth penetrates I penetrate these cities myself, / All islands to which birds wing their way I wing my way myself."

Closely related to this presentation of consciousness in terms of the "moment" is Whitman's constant use of the present participle, which is another device for extricating "action" from the temporal frame and realizing it as a mode of being, an aspect of eternity. The present participle is the patent device by which Whitman dramatizes or enacts experience and presents events in the only way in which human consciousness can grasp them—as a living experience. Most of Whitman's lines owe their lyric power to this dramatizing of emotion in terms of the participle. Whitman's mind habitually operates by blurring the sense of time and reducing all events to the living present. Thus, the poem "Out of the Cradle" is a reminiscence, but it has a dramatic, not a narrative form, for the poet presents a past event dramatically by enacting it as a living emotion. The passage which begins: "The aria sinking" is a magnificent train of present participles moving with a cumulative strength; it demonstrates the skill with which the poet exploits the power of this device. "After the Sea-Ship" (Sea-Drift), "Patrolling Barnegat" (Sea-Drift), and "The Dalliance of the Eagles" (By the Roadside) are other remarkable instances in which experience is rendered imagistically purely in terms of the present participle. On the other hand, the narrative passages in which he merely reports events in the past tense are generally lacking in this lyric power, like the accounts of the "jetblack sunrise" and the "frigate-fight" (Sections 34, 35, "Song of Myself"), which read like dull narratives and are out of accord with the exultant tone of the poem. But Section 36 recovers the strength of the narrative as the thick crowding of appositional passages rushes on with a mounting climactic force toward a structural conclusion in the line: "These so, these irretrievable."

The result of "intuitive identity" is achieved by other devices in the poems. Whitman's verb-negating statements[67] obliterate clear

[67] See Jean Catel, *Rythme et langage dans la 1re Edition du Leaves of Grass* (Paris: Les Editions Reider, 1930). "Me Imperturbe" ("Inscriptions") and "Spontaneous Me" ("Children of Adam") are remarkable for the negation of the verb in the principal sentence. Both the poems build through a bold series of rhetorical imperatives to present a portrait of the "Me."

grammatical connections, along with subject-object "relationship," and establish "identity." The verb, by the very nature of its function, is an instrument of mediation, the middle category in the Hegelian triad. I have pointed out that the paradoxical form is the characteristic form in which the mystic's unitive consciousness is affirmed. The classic example of this paradoxical affirmation is Emerson's "Brahma," which suggests close parallels to the verses of the Bhagavad Gita. The paradox in the poem is the paradox of the intuitional self, which is at once subject and object and which leaps over the distinction between the two.

> Far and forgot to me is near;
> Shadow and sunlight are the same;
> The vanished gods to me appear;
> And one to me are shame and fame.
> They reckon ill who leave me out;
> When me they fly, I am the wings;
> I am the doubter and the doubt,
> And I am the hymn the Brahmin sings.

The experiencing subject is the indivisible self and is at once the actor, action, and the instruments of action. Like the cosmic Krishna in the Gita (9.16, 19): "I am the ritual action, I am the sacrifice, I am the ancestral oblation, I am the sacred hymn, I am also the melted butter, I am the fire and I am the offering. I am immortality and also death, I am being as well as non-being. . . ."

The spirit of paradox informs many of Whitman's lines and is a major stylistic device in his verse. Whitman's successful exploitation of the paradoxical style is seen in two short poems entitled "A Riddle Song" and "Great Are the Myths."

> That which eludes this verse and any verse,
> Unheard by sharpest ear, unform'd in clearest eye or cunningest
>    mind,
> Nor lore nor fame, nor happiness nor wealth,
> And yet the pulse of every heart and life throughout the world
>    incessantly,
> Which you and I and all pursuing ever ever miss,
> Open but still a secret, the real of the real, an illusion,
> Costless, vouchsafed to each, yet never the man the owner,

Which poets vainly seek to put in rhyme, historians in prose,

. . . . . . . . . . .

Invoking here and now I challenge for my song.[68]

These lines recall to mind the description of the *brahman* in the Upanishads in negative and paradoxical terms. "Great Are the Myths" is another such poem which is deliberately paradoxical in expression and import. In this the poet equates the polarized notions of life and death, good and evil, youth and old age, riches and poverty in a series of dramatic utterances.

Great is Youth—equally great is Old Age—great are the Day and
    Night;
Great is Wealth—great is Poverty—great is Expression—great is
    Silence.
Great is goodness;
. . . . .
Great is wickedness. . . .
Do you call that a paradox? It certainly is a paradox.
The eternal equilibrium of things is great, and the eternal overthrow
    of things is great,
And there is another paradox.

The "Song of Myself" makes the largest use of the paradoxical expression; there are about thirty-seven paradoxical pairs in it on a rough count. While the poem as a whole moves within the paradoxical framework set up by the opening lines:

I celebrate myself, and sing myself,
And what I assume you shall assume,
For every atom belonging to me as good belongs to you,

it brings together all pairs of opposites (*dvandvās*) in a paradoxical conjunction and negates them. Thus, the paradoxes are subject-object–difference negating, time- and space-negating (the sense of up and

[68] "A Riddle Song," in "From Noon to Starry Night." The real purport of this poem is rather difficult to ascertain as Whitman does not give the key to its "riddle." The first twenty and the last three lines would seem to fit the description (in paradoxical terms) of the elusive and ubiquitous self, of which he speaks elsewhere. The rest of the lines in which he says: "How justified by it, the horrors, evils, battles of the earth!" recall to mind the poem "To Thee Old Cause" ("Inscriptions"). See Holloway, *op. cit.*, p. 1079, note on the poem.

down, behind and before, far and near), death- and life-negating, good- and evil-negating, etc. This antithetical parallelism is, thus, a most important element of the rhythmical style of the poems we have considered.

Whitman's conception of democracy is also expressed in paradoxical terms. The antithetical concepts of "completeness in separation" and the human aggregate are fused in the concept of identity or personalism.[69] What might look like a triadic structure in Whitman's poems is in fact a paradoxical form, in which the polarities of thought meet in conjunction and negate each other. Thus, the antinomies or pairs of opposites of life and death, joy and sorrow, good and evil, body and soul, matter and spirit are brought together and consumed in the burning glass of paradoxical relationship. Alfred H. Marks,[70] in his provocative article, has tried to interpret Whitman's poetry in terms of the dialectical triad. In Whitman's poetry he finds a form of Hegel-like logic with which the poet "seems deliberately to cultivate the attainment of both poles simultaneously in order to mediate dramatically between the extremes." According to him, both Whitman and Emerson make use of "the logical technique which Hegel popularized, the Dialectic," and the unity that Whitman achieves is the equivalent of the Hegelian synthesis which "contains" the contradictions of the opposite terms of body and soul, etc. Marks says, "Many of the poems in *Leaves of Grass* depend greatly upon the triadic technique for their structure." And so do Emerson's major essays illustrate this logic, in Mark's opinion. Obviously, he fails to observe in both Emerson's and Whitman's writings the logic which lies deeper than the apparent dialectic form which they may exhibit at first sight. A great deal of Emerson's thought, in fact, the most essential part of it, is not dialectical but intuitive in its implications. We have already examined some manifestations of this intuition in his

[69] "Personalism fuses this," "Democratic Vistas," Holloway, *op. cit.*, p. 693. Whitman's use of this term in this essay is not to be interpreted in the same sense in which Bronson Alcott employed it to designate his own conception of a divine person. Rather, the term should be understood in the sense of an inclusive identity of the self, developed more fully in "Song of Myself." "This second principle is individuality, the pride and centripetal isolation of a human being in himself— identity—personalism." Holloway, *op. cit.*, p. 687. See also Gay Wilson Allen, *The Solitary Singer* (New York: Macmillan Co., 1955), p. 393.

[70] "Whitman's Triadic Imagery," *American Literature*, XXIII (March, 1951), 99–126.

lines, and in his poem "Brahma." Emerson's essays do, no doubt, contain discussions of "polarities," but this polar logic is confined only to nature and the world of phenomena, as Emerson sees it, while the soul remains an identity, removed from all contradictions. The following statement from "Compensation" should clarify the issue. While "polarity, or action and reaction, we meet in every part of nature" and the universe is governed by the law of compensation,

> There is a deeper fact in the soul than compensation, to wit, its own nature. The soul is not a compensation, but a life. The soul is. Under all this running sea of circumstance, whose waters ebb and flow with perfect balance, lies the aboriginal abyss of real Being. Essence, or God, is not a relation or a part, but the whole. Being is the vast affirmative, excluding negation, self-balanced, and swallowing up all relations, parts and times within itself.

It will be difficult to read dialectical meanings into a passage like this. The conception here is clearly that of a being or pure existence that is not a Hegelian synthesis of antithetical terms. It is not necessary to labor the point any further; the whole purport of this essay has been to show that the method by which Whitman negotiates with the world of objects is not dialectical mediation between the poles, but a dramatic transposition of them, that is, the method of intuitive identification. The form in which this identity is expressed is the paradox, and not the dialectical triad.

No doubt, some of Whitman's lines have an apparent triadic structure, in the manner of Hegel's "curious triplicate process," which fascinated Whitman, particularly in his later days, but there is no mistake about their implication. Let us take a typical triadic image, which in the opinion cited above is illustrative of the theme of the "triadic self." "I too with my soul and body / We, a curious trio. . . ." Here the trio is not a dialectical synthesis, but just a dramatization of the body-soul identity. The "I" is the grammatical subject, the speaker, that is, the poet, reporting to us, and is not considered as being apart from the soul. This point is borne out more clearly in the following lines: "Come, said my soul. / Such verses for my body let us write (for we are one)." The implication of the last line is clearly paradoxical, for it means that verses written for the body are verses written for the soul, because of the assumption that body and soul are one. Let us examine another such triadic image.

> My comrade!
> For you to share with me two greatnesses, and a third one rising inclusive and more resplendent,
> The greatness of love and Democracy, and the greatness of Religion.[71]

Love and democracy are not antithetical concepts embraced and reconciled in religion, which is the synthesis. Rather, they are both given in the self as corollaries to its spiritual nature—which is religion. The self is what expresses itself in love and makes democracy possible. We may turn this round and say that all the three concepts are implied in any one of them, so that given one we have the others; and each of them is a paradox. Thus, love, which is the give-and-take, separateness-merger paradox is also the individual-aggregate paradox of democracy, and the one-and-many, self-and-not-self paradox of identity, which is religion. But of this conception of the self as the paradox of identity I shall speak in the next chapter.

R. P. Adams has examined Whitman and Emerson in the light of the organic metaphor.[72] In his own words, this metaphor "embodies the concept of progressive relatedness and ultimate unity. . . ." The organic metaphor establishes a new conception of the structure of reality—a system of functional relationships and no thing-in-itself. "The goal of everything is growth, development, progressively higher and more complex organization." Whitman, no doubt, believes in the organic unity of life and in growth conceived both as a process of increasing enrichment of all life and a mode of dynamic being. He also shares in the Romantic theory of art as an organic expression acting under "laws of its own origination." But, paradoxically, he also assumes the existence of an unchanging, non-dimensional unity in human consciousness. Furthermore his universe, though marching dynamically governed by the law of "transfers and promotions,"[73] is not an organization of complex relationships, but one in which

---

[71] "Starting from Paumanok," 10.

[72] "Whitman: A Brief Revaluation," *Tulane Studies in English*, V (1955), 111–49; "Emerson and the Organic Metaphor," in Feidelson and Brodtkorb, *op, cit.*, pp. 137–51.

[73] "O perpetual transfers and promotions," "Song of Myself," 49.

things are ever "merging" and "flowing," forever remaining the same, and forever remaining unique in the eternal now. The clue to Whitman's poetry is this presentation of life and experience summed up in the existent object in itself, regardless of its "relationships," and in the instant of consciousness, respectively.

Not only does Adams define organicism in terms of the dialectic, he sees the dialectic as the operating principle in Whitman's poetry. He says, "The structural principle in Whitman's poems proceeds by the method of reconciling opposites which Coleridge recommended and Hegel systematized. The main lines on which he builds are those connecting the polar opposites of the individual and society, man and nature, body and soul, matter and spirit, life and death. . . . In each case, it is on the relation between the opposites, as relation, that he mainly focuses his attention in his thought and his art." "Whitman's use of these opposites is genuinely dialectical." Adams is right in pointing out that Whitman's poetic effort is directed toward building up a sense of total unity; but, as I have contended, the method by which the poet achieves this effect is not the dialectic, but the mystic paradox in which the polar opposites, instead of being "balanced" are fused and dissolved. Nor is this unity, in which, according to Whitman, all things are fused, an "organization" or a complex system of relations in which diversities are included and integrated by progressive steps. On the other hand, it is a mystic "float"—a state of solution such as is symbolized in "Crossing Brooklyn Ferry," or a pervasive sense of undifferentiated oneness symbolized in "The Sleepers." Adams further observes in Whitman's catalogues the operation of the dialectical principle and finds in them imagery that is "dialectically developed." It is difficult to trace in the catalogues any such dialectic development. As I have pointed out before, Whitman's imagery builds "cumulatively," not "dialectically," or with one image giving rise to its opposite, and the two together being enfolded in a third. The principle of its growth is its symbolic fusion with the self. Thus, any given catalogue in "Song of Myself," for instance, does not present a complex organization or tissue of relations—dialectical or otherwise—for the images do not function in relation to one another, except that sometimes they grow out of the free association of ideas; it presents a patch of telescoped experience, as it were, constantly related to the "omnific" principle of the "I." A close examination of

Sections 8, 15, and 33, which are typical examples of Whitman's catalogues will bear this out. Thus, in the following enumeration from Section 15,

> The pure contralto sings in the organ loft,
> The carpenter dresses his plank ...
> The married and unmarried children ride home to their Thanksgiving
>     dinner,

there is no conceivable relation between the "pure contralto," the carpenter and the children riding home, except that these separate, and independently meaningful, strands of images are connected to the "enveloping" vision of the "I": "And these one and all tend inward to me, and I tend outward to them, / And such as it is to be of these more or less I am." Evidently what Whitman is trying to do in his catalogues is to capture the essence of existence in the single object, and capture experience itself in the single instant or "fact of consciousness," and unite these enumerated objects and instants, not in any complex texture of relationships, but in the paradoxical entity of the *One that is the Many*—which is no other than the "omnific" I of "Song of Myself."

At this point we must restate the distinction between the dialectical and the paradoxical forms. The basic assumptions of the dialectic are two: that opposites are united through mediation, and that they are progressively united in larger and more complex "integrations" through the "pyramid of hierarchical mountings," as Kenneth Burke has put it. The basic implication of the paradox is that logical opposites, being asserted simultaneously nullify each other, thus affirming non-opposition. The oxymoron, as a figure, to quote Kenneth Burke's definition,[74] has a dialectic form in which the contradictory elements (like those in "cruel kindness") exist simultaneously as persons of a single unity without annihilating each other. Burke sees the principle of the oxymoron as the characteristic form of mystical consciousness[75] and leaves out of consideration the operation of the principle of the paradox. This is, of course, perfectly consistent with Burke's philo-

[74] "Mysticism as a Solution to the Poet's Dilemma," in Stanley Romain Hopper, *Spiritual Problems in Contemporary Literature* (New York: Institute for Religious and Social Studies, 1952).
[75] *A Rhetoric of Motives* (New York: Prentice-Hall, 1950), p. 324.

sophy of "dramatism," which with its Hegelian assumptions necessarily commits him to the logic of dialectic. Hence, Burke finds in the oxymoron the rhetorical form of the dialectic and shows no proper appreciation of the implications of the paradox.

# CHAPTER THREE

# Emergent Ego

*... the mystical identity the real I or Me or You*
*(Complete Writings, Vol. VI, Part I, No. 28)*

Any consistent interpretation of Whitman should, in my opinion, be centered around the concept of self, for the self is at once the organizing principle in his poetry and the stuff of the experience that it dramatizes. This unity of theme corresponds to a central identity of experience, which the poet finds in the very nature of consciousness itself. All unity is to be sought within the self, as all consciousness is the consciousness of self. The problem of the poet-mystic is to construct a cosmos out of "this multifarious mad chaos" and achieve inner and outer unity. To Whitman this principle of unity lies in his own self. It is not an outside fact. Here, the native egotism of the man might have induced him to seek unity within his own self, instead of seeking it outside. The "colossal egoism" of "Song of Myself," which has puzzled many of his students and evoked the odium of his critics, is the key to the man and his work. For Whitman the "I" is the very center and meaning of all existence.[1] This egotistical disposition also explains the attraction of idealism for Whitman and his advocacy of it as the proper guide and base of New World metaphysics.[2] Whitman's own spiritual experiences induced him to think that the clue to the world lay in his own self and that reality itself was not different from the self. Idealism gave intellectual sanction to his convictions, as it sought to explain the nature of things by reference to the self of man, and by making him the center of the universe. In "A Backward Glance" Whitman writes; "In the center of all, and object of all, stands the human being, towards whose heroic and spiritual evolution

[1] Cf. Emerson: "I—this thought which is called I—is the mould in which the world is poured like melted wax" ("The Transcendentalist").
[2] See "Democratic Vistas," *Complete Poetry and Selected Prose and Letters*, edited by Emory Holloway (London: Nonesuch Press, 1938), p. 713.

poems and everything directly and indirectly tend, Old World or New.[3]

The conception that man is the master and measure of all things, no doubt, goes back to the Greek philosophers; but, as we have seen, it is in the post-Kantian idealistic systems that it emerges as a definite doctrine of self. Fichte, Schelling, and Hegel constructed a metaphysic after the pattern of the self. Fichte saw the ego as the ultimate reality, and the world as its creation. Schelling, too, referred all existence to self-consciousness. To Hegel the self is the absolute. But, since for all these philosophers dialectic is the vehicle of their thought, their conception of self is also dialectical. The self is a dialectical and antithetical being to which dualism and opposition become a necessary condition of existence. The Fichtean ego conceives itself as opposed by a not-ego in order to realize itself as ego or intelligence, and the world is the product of its self-conscious activity. Schelling's self, too, is thus committed to an internal differentiation, for the self, to be a self-knower, has to determine itself by an object. Its ideal or infinite aspect depends on its real or finite aspect. Hegel made opposition the principle of creation and transcendence. The self subsists by subduing the opposition of the not-self. Nature is an obstacle, a necessary obstacle, or an inferior phase of the spirit, or at best it is an instrument which the absolute exploits for its own needs. Neither is the individual's position assured. Though for these dialecticians self is the principle of their philosophy, this self is not the self of all, but a superarrogant absolute standing above our heads. The individuals are instruments subserving the absolute purpose. Reality is, thus, an external fact existing in superaddition to the individual selves. If, however, the individual fancied that he was the absolute, whole and undivided, it would be, in the opinion of our idealists, an unpardonable presumption.

Whitman's essentially mystical thinking would be opposed to any doctrine that accords to the individual but a dependent and inferior status. Whitman asserts, "And nothing, not God, is greater to one than one's self is."[4] A true doctrine of self is that which holds that the individual is coeval and coeternal with the absolute and accords to every particle of the universe the status of the supreme. This attitude is expressed in the well-known passage of the Upanishads, "The Whole

[3] *Ibid.*, p. 866.
[4] "Song of Myself," 48.

is all That. The Whole is all This. The Whole is born out of the Whole. When the Whole is absorbed into the Whole the Whole alone remains."[5] It is the Upanishads that develop a supreme doctrine of self. It is true that in the Plotinian system, too, the individual soul is assumed to be the all-soul complete. However, it is in the Upanishads that this emphasis and the approach to reality from the inner principle of the self is most clearly developed. The Upanishadic system conceives reality on the pattern of the inner core or *atman*, the permanent substance which remains immutable and identical amidst the changing panorama of the outer world. This *atman* or soul is the internal *atman* of all created things (*sarvabhūtāntarātmā*), and as such the only unifying principle in the world. The opposition of the not-self which confronts the self at every step is not its own wilful creation, nor a necessity—in which case it would be impossible to transcend—but the result of an unreal self-limitation on the part of the self. Unity is established when the self gets to know itself and eradicates the wrong belief in its limitation. Finitude is the outcome of man's limited vision; man can realize the limitlessness of his nature by enlarging his consciousness. The way to attain this vision is by growing into our surroundings, as it were, through an interpenetration of our being into all objects. Nature is not an antithesis of spirit, nor is it an inferior term, but it exists as it is, as the immortal Brahman. "All this universe has sprung from immortal life and is vibrating with life.[6] The Upanishads express the view that nature is not merely "spirit unconscious," as Schelling assumed, but is itself intelligence and immortal Brahman.[7] Since self is the reality and since it is identical with the universe, recognition of its real nature is the ultimate end and fulfilment of life. To be one's own self is to establish unity with the all.

## II

Whitman's intense self-awareness might have sprung from the early autoerotic emotions of his boyhood and a primary narcissism. But it manifested itself as a certain habit of mentally returning upon himself,

[5] Brihadaranyaka Upanishad, 5.1.

[6] Katha Upanishad, 6.2.

[7] There is no difference even in degree between the conscious spirit of man and nature. The Upanishads do not recognize any dualism between matter and intelligence. Matter itself is God.

of reflecting upon his own inner processes. Whitman was a dreamy boy, a languid mystical type, with a lazy, contemplative habit of mind. He was exceptionally susceptible to his physical and spiritual environment. His own mystical inclination was aided by the strong religious proclivities of his paternal family, who were followers of Quakerism, and the boy's early training, in the belief in "inner light," made him all the more receptive to "quietism" and predisposed him to a mystical life. The "child" who went forth every day becoming the object he looked upon showed a wonderful capacity for intuitive identification. "The Sleepers" describes the poet's habit, going back to his early boyhood, of living in a visionary world, identifying himself with the life and objects around—a habit he continued into his maturity; the poem offers a key to Whitman's poetic genesis. Whitman's boundless love of life together with a natural vigor and fulness of spirit, made him seek warm, living contact with the stuff of life. And his education among the elemental forces of nature, the ocean, the daylight, the woods, increased this tendency to mystical communion. He was to express this later in the lines:

> In me the caresser of life wherever moving, backward as well as
> forward sluing,
> To niches aside and junior bending, nor a person or object missing,
> Absorbing all to myself and for this song.[8]

Even from his early boyhood Whitman seems to have felt intuitively that nature and the world of objects were in some sense "flowing" or "fluid" and that between himself and the universe there was an intercommunion. The "child" who became part of the objects and of whom the objects became a part felt no barriers between the universe and his soul, each flowed into the other, each interpenetrated the other. In men and nature he saw the same essence or life and spoke of them and contacted them with equal enthusiasm. Whitman's interest in the teeming life of New York on the one hand, and in the natural objects of the seaside, where his birthplace was, continued side by side, and he retained this wholesome balance till his death. This was so because his instincts revealed to him the unity of life everywhere, and his later meditations confirmed this.

For over ten years before 1855, Whitman sauntered about in New

---

[8] "Song of Myself," 13.

York, watching men and things and charmed by the panorama of life in the city, the crowds, the shops, the theaters. Yet, this was no young beast "wallowing in the stream of his sensibilia,"[9] flooded by the phantasmagoria of continuous visions and images, for the youth who appeared so deeply absorbed in the moving world around had no tendency to be obsessed by it. Walking Broadway, riding the omnibus tops, or watching the crowds in the streets, he was watching his own self; he was all the time aware of himself as walking, riding, moving. He had an unusual capacity for standing aloof while in the midst of the crowd, to ponder, to contemplate the seething life. He had a capacity for both intuitive identification and mystical abstraction, "Or withdrawn to muse and meditate in some deep recess, / Far from the clank of crowds intervals passing rapt and happy."[10] It was also this capacity for abstracting from his surroundings that was, as his mind matured, to give him an insight into his own real nature and show it to be different from the outer forms and shows. But this realization was to come to him only by an active responsiveness to the surge of life, by participation and mergence in the great life of the all. "As for me," Whitman said,

> I blessed my lucky stars; for merely to sail—to lie on my back and gaze by the half-hour at the passing clouds overhead—merely to breathe and live in the sweet air and clear sunlight—to hear the musical clatter of girls as they pursued their own glee,—was happiness enough for one day—there is an ecstatic satisfaction in such lazy philosophy, such passive yielding up of one's self to the pure emanation of nature, better than the most exciting pleasures.[11]

This indicates a mind framed at once for passive receptivity and intense self-awareness, a heart alive both to the "influx" and the "efflux," absorbing that which flows from without and that which wells from within.

The years between 1838 and 1855, when Whitman lived in Brooklyn and New York, absorbing the life of the cities with great avidity, were years of unusual activity in Whitman's life, and formed the special

[9] George Santayana, *Interpretations of Poetry and Religion* (New York: Charles Scribner's Sons, 1916), p. 180.

[10] "Starting from Paumanok," 1.

[11] Quoted in Emory Holloway, *Whitman: An Interpretation in Narrative* (New York: Alfred A. Knopf, 1926), p. 190.

gestation period of the *Leaves*.[12] Whitman is reported to have said of his work: "Remember, the book arose out of my life in Brooklyn and New York from 1838 to 1855, absorbing a million people with an intimacy, an eagerness, an abandon, probably never equaled."[13] These were also years of intense spiritual activity, when Whitman, perhaps goaded by the deep emotional needs natural to youth, started upon the path of self-quest, though it was not until about 1847–48, following a long process of spiritual incubation, that he was to attain a true knowledge of himself. Whitman's writings of this period, though as literary compositions they sound banal and amateurish, are of immense significance for his spiritual history because they reveal a mind in turmoil, a torn soul, tormented by doubts and uncertainties, struggling to free itself from its own cravings. The restlessness and travail that his juvenile poems betray were the signs of the spirit's growth, the birth throes of a new life. Through these conflicts we discover the aspiring soul. Here is a poem published in 1838:

> This breast which now alternate burns
> With flashing hope and gloomy fear,
> Where beats a heart that knows the hue
> Which aching bosoms wear;
> This curious frame of human mold,
> Where craving wants unceasing play
> The troubled heart and wondrous form
> Must both alike decay.
> The close wet earth will close around
> Dull senseless limbs and a shy face,
> But where, O Nature! where will be
> My mind's abiding place?
> Will it even live? For though its light
> Must shine till from the body torn;
> Then when the oil of life is spent,
> Still shall the taper burn?
> O, Powerless is this struggling brain
> To pierce the mighty mystery;

[12] For excellent reconstructions of this period in Whitman's biography, see Gay Wilson Allen, *The Solitary Singer* (New York: Macmillan Co., 1955), H. S. Canby, *Walt Whitman: An American* (Boston: Houghton Mifflin Co., 1943), and Emory Holloway, *Whitman*.

[13] Quoted in the *Complete Writings of Walt Whitman* (New York: G. P. Putnam's Sons, 1902), VII, Part IV, 103.

In dark, uncertain awe it waits,
The common doom to die!
Mortal can thy swelling soul
Live with the thought that all its life
Is centered in this earthly cage
Of care, and tears, and life?
Not so, that sorrowing heart of thine
Ere long will find a house of rest;
Thy form, repurified shall rise,
In robes of beauty drest.
The flickering taper's glow shall change
To bright and star-like majesty,
Radiant with pure and piercing light
From the Eternal's eye.[14]

This reveals how seriously the nineteen-year-old boy was pondering on the great mysteries of human life and death. Human mortality presented to him a baffling problem. He was convinced that worldly ambition and fame were vanities of vanities because they were forms of death,[15] and belonged to man's finite existence. The same meditations on death, the vanity of ambition and fame recur in his other poems written during the same period.[16] "My Departure" (1839) reveals the poet's spirit struggling to free itself from the trammels of flesh.

O mighty powers of Destiny!
When from this coil of flesh I'm free—
When through my second life I rove,
Let me but find one heart to love,
As I would wish to love.
For vainly through this world below
We seek affection. Nought but woe
Is with our earthly journey wove,
And so the heart must look above,
Or die in dull despair.[17]

Earthly love too is perishable; it is a bondage. The poet has, however,

[14] "Our Future Lot," *Uncollected Poetry and Prose*, edited by Emory Holloway (New York: Doubleday, Doran & Co., 1922), Vol. I.
[15] "*mṛtyōh rūpāṇi*", Brihadaranyaka, 4.3.7.
[16] "Fame's Vanity" (1839), "Ambition" (1842), "The Love That Is Hereafter" (1840), "End of All" (1840). See Holloway, *op. cit.*, Vol. I.
[17] Holloway, *op. cit.*, Vol. I.

a vague intuition of an existence freed from the bondage of matter. Spiritual activity begins with a dissatisfaction with the transient values of the world and a craving for the permanent. The capacity to discriminate between the eternal and the non-eternal is an essential qualification of the seeker of wisdom. Nachiketas in the Katha Upanishad refuses to be tempted by the offer by Yama (the god of the underworld) of worldly wealth and happiness. "Like corn decays the mortal and like corn is born again."[18] "What are these riches to me," asks Maitreyi in the Brihadaranyaka, "If I am not thereby to gain life eternal?"[19] The desire for immortality is the starting point of metaphysics; in the Brihadaranyaka metaphysical inquiry begins with the craving for eternal life. "But where, O Nature! Where will be / My mind's abiding place?" is the cry of Whitman's spirit. The poet had to wait before he could discover the heart of the mystery, but constant meditation seemed for the while to bear fruit. In a paper written in 1840 Whitman recorded a change that had come over him, a new sense and an altered point of view:

> a wondrous and important discovery . . . I have found that it is a very dangerous thing to be rich. For a considerable time past this idea has been pressing upon me and I am now fully and unalterably convinced of its truth. Some years ago when my judgement was in the bud I thought that riches were desirable things. But I have altered my mind. Light had flowed in upon me . . . the mists and clouds have cleared away, and I can now behold things as they really are.[20]

The cosmic sense had begun to grow in upon him. Money symbolizes man's hankering after what is finite and perishable; worldly possessions are limitations set upon the spirit. Because of a wrong identification the poet's soul had been cherishing false values. But now the veil of ignorance had cleared away; he could behold things in their true perspective. Another paper written in the same year shows the eager soul in search of truth. Whitman wrote:

> I reflected on the folly and vanity of those objects with which most men occupy their lives; and the awe and dread with which they approach its close. I remembered the strife for temporary and puerile distinctions— the seeking after useless and cumbersome wealth—the yielding up the

18 Katha, 1.6.
19 Brihadaranyaka, 2.4.3.
20 Sun-Down Papers, No. 7 (1840), Holloway, *op. cit.*, Vol. I.

diseased mind to be a prey to constant melancholy and discontent; all which may be daily seen by those who have intercourse with the sons of man.[21]

Whitman's experience of the world had convinced him of "the littleness of all earthly achievements."[22] He had realized the true value of renunciation; and true renunciation consists in the rejection of the unstable and a dedication to the eternal. The Katha says,

> The childish go after outward pleasure;
> They walk into the net of widespread death,
> But the wise, knowing immortality,
> Seek not the stable among things, which are unstable here.[23]

Spiritual life starts with a transformation of values. But this, as yet, is the beginning. Renunciation is but a prelude in the life of the aspirant. The supreme sense of fulfilment and peace, which is the goal of the mystic quest, had not yet come to Whitman. The highest truth, namely the self, still remained to be discovered. But this could only be accomplished through an arduous psychological process, entailing the complete remaking of character, a purging of the dross, as it were.[24]

In "Morbid Appetite for Money" Whitman wrote, "On no particular matter is the public mind more unhealthy than the appetite for money."[25] More dreadful than poverty was the "poverty of soul," by which the wealthy were afflicted. Really sublime and grand characters were those who loved silent and unknown without the desire for fame. Whitman spoke of "enjoying the treasures of soul inherent within." A new sense of values was impinging on him; and here are clear indications that the poet's gaze was turning more and more inward. Whitman was beginning to see that "self-reliance" might be the clue to the "curious abrupt questionings"[26] that were stirring within him, but the vision was still inchoate and needed greater clarifying. As the editor of the Brooklyn *Daily Eagle*, Whitman was engaged in the political controversies of his time. But though thus

[21] *Ibid.*, No. 8.
[22] *Ibid.*
[23] Katha, 4.2.
[24] See Evelyn Underhill, *Mysticism: A Study in the Nature and Development of Man's Spiritual Consciousness* (London: Methuen & Co., Ltd., 1919). p. 96.
[25] Holloway, *op. cit.*, I, 123.
[26] "Crossing Brooklyn Ferry," 5.

seriously employed with politics and social reform, Whitman still had time for inner communings. In the midst of his journalistic activities Whitman would snatch an hour or two for a stroll or a swim. Or he would go into the solitary retreats of nature and sit by a pond-side, brooding. The following lines, though written actually during a later period, give us a glimpse into Whitman's inner life and habits.

> In paths untrodden
> In the growth by margins of pond-waters,
> Escaped from the life that exhibits itself,
> From all the standards hitherto published, from the pleasures, profits, conformities,
> Which too long I was offering to feed my soul,
> Clear to me now standards not yet publish'd . . .
> . . . . . . . . . .
> Here by myself away from the clank of the world . . .
> . . . . . . . . . .
> Strong upon me the life that does not exhibit itself, yet contains all the rest.[27]

His inner life was not, however, growing in opposition to the outer. All the time he was engaged in politics and journalism, Whitman was living intensely, thinking and understanding. The life around him was the very stuff of his contemplation, and he had a genius for turning everything to spiritual account and making it food for his thought. Whitman had learned to appreciate the worthlessness of worldly pursuits and possessions; hence, he was not to be engrossed by them. But he had not won the fight for self-mastery. His nature was torn by an internal dualism; his spirit was restive under the bondage of matter. The senses claimed their toll. The consciousness of human mortality haunted him like a nightmare. In his manuscript notebook dated 1847–48 he noted down:

> I am not glad tonight. Gloom has gathered round me like a mantle tightly folded. Yet I know not why I should be sad. Around me are my brother men merry and jovial. No dear one is in danger. . . . Thus comes that I am not glad tonight. I feel cramped in these coarse walls of flesh. The soul disdains. . . . O mystery of death I pant for the time when I shall solve you.[28]

These notebook jottings give evidences of deep emotional experiences

[27] "In Paths Untrodden," in "Calamus."
[28] Holloway, *op. cit.*, II, 89.

that Whitman might have gone through during these years. But these experiences revealed to him mysterious depths within himself and brought him to a keener consciousness of himself. The floodgates of a sexually passionate nature, the "Pent-up aching rivers"[29] of himself gave way. Whitman later dramatized his fight for self-mastery in these lines of "Song of Myself":

> I am given up by traitors,
> I talk wildly, I have lost my wits, I and nobody else am the greatest traitor,
> I went myself first to the headland, my own hands carried me there.
> You villain touch! What are you doing? . . . .
> Unclench your floodgates, you are too much for me.[30]

Whitman had not yet realized that he had all the while been laboring under a false notion, a wrong identification; all sense of conflict is a mere illusion superimposed on the soul. Whitman was in fact fighting a contrary tendency within his own self. He was in need of some clue, some guidance, or some philosophy which would aid and precipitate the internal activity of his mind. His conflicts and unrest were due to the heterogeneousness of his nature. His personality had to be integrated, his inner self unified. And this would not be achieved so long as the sense of duality continued. The self must get to know its identity and its expansive nature.

During the years before the composition of the first *Leaves* Whitman passed through a phase of self-instruction. He was an indefatigable reader and the range of his knowledge was extraordinary, if judged by his preparatory reading and thought. Whitman read widely, doubtless pursuing some clue for his own inner life. He, like Emerson, "regarded reading as a creative activity."[31] In an article entitled "Thoughts on Reading" in the May, 1845, issue of the *American Whig Review*, Whitman underscored, "An author enriches us, not so much by giving us his ideas, as by unfolding in us the same powers that originated them."[32] Reading clarified his own native visions and confirmed his intuitions.

Of all the diverse thought currents and intellectual movements which moulded Whitman's poetic faith during these years, the young

[29] "Children of Adam."
[30] "Song of Myself," 28; see also Holloway, *op. cit.*, II, 73.
[31] Allen, *The Solitary Singer*, p. 126.
[32] Quoted from *The Solitary Singer*, p. 126.

America movement and the *Democratic Review*, Epicurean and Stoic ideas,[33] to mention but a few of them, the most influential in the shaping of his mind and art were the "transcendental" ideas of Emerson and *Dial* magazine. Whitman's acquaintance with Emerson's works probably began about 1847, for in that year he reviewed Emerson's "Spiritual Laws." This date is significant because about the same time, probably, Whitman underwent a spiritual "conversion." The growing pressure within compelled him to search for spiritual guidance. He attended "Swedenborg meetings." He was roused to know more and more about the peoples of the world and their thoughts. India, Palestine, and Egypt attracted his imagination, and he seems to have read about their literatures, at least superficially, in magazine articles. Above all was the transcendental philosophy of Emerson which proved of inestimable value to Whitman's spiritual growth. "The same, the same,"[34] Emerson wrote, quoting from the Hindu scriptures, "without identity at base chaos must be forever." The soul is the "one Bottom," the universal ground. Echoing the Upanishads, he said, "For it is only the finite that has wrought and suffered; the infinite lies stretched in smiling repose."[35] He emphasized the importance of self-knowledge. "Trust Thyself," he said, by which he meant "Know thyself and be thyself," for the soul is limitless and free. No laws can circumscribe it; it exists on its own strength. Conflict, unhappiness, and mortality belong to finite existence and are not of the real nature of the self. Man sees the world broken because he is broken within. What a revelation it must have been to the toiling soul of Whitman! Here was a philosophy that answered to his deepest cravings. Here was the solution he had been struggling to find. Emerson's transcendentalism offered him light at a time when he was passing through a crisis of development. Emerson helped him to "find himself." "I was simmering, simmering, simmering," Whitman said; "Emerson brought me to a boil." Emerson's essays provided the needed precipitant. What had been in a state of subconscious incubation was now brought to consciousness. Whitman, had, at last, found the self.

[33] For a discussion of the literary influences on Whitman, see *The Solitary Singer*, chap. iv.

[34] "Plato" (1850).

[35] "Spiritual Laws." Cf., Chhandogya Upanishad, 7.23.1, "The Infinite is bliss; there is no bliss in what is small."

The year 1847/48 marked the new birth. "A remarkable accession of power," an enlargement and clarification of vision had come to Whitman. He recorded this astounding discovery and new spirit in his notebook (No. 1), which contains a clear, though half-articulate, adumbration of "Song of Myself." Through his emotional turmoil Whitman had come out spiritually emergent. By constant brooding and meditation and self-mastery, and by the practice of discrimination, Whitman had come to know his real self and realize it in its glory. For the first time in the writings of this period we come across this utterance: "I cannot understand the mystery, but I am always conscious of myself as two—as my soul and I and I reckon it is the same with all men and women." [36] The soul is the transcendental self, the "I," the surface consciousness, or the empirical ego—which is falsely identified with the objects and experiences of the world. Ignorance consists in confounding the one with the other, in the superposition of the object on the subject (*ātmani anātmādhyāsa*). Discrimination between the two is the starting point as well as the end of all knowledge. The Gita says: "Those who perceive by their eye of wisdom the distinction between the Field (nature, not-self) and the Knower of the field (transcendental subject, the witness) attain to the Supreme. This knowledge is the true knowledge." [37] And Whitman had gained this. He had also realized that his "soul" is the "universal and fluid soul." [38] The result of this knowledge is the termination of bondage and an unobstructed expansion of the soul and its identification with all existence.

> The soul or spirit transmits itself into all matter, into rocks and can live the life of a rock—into the sea, and can feel itself the sea—into the oak . . . into an animal, and feel itself a horse, a fish or bird, into the earth —into the motions of sun and stars. [39]

With this self-expansion Whitman felt that the ubiquitous soul of man enters into all existence and bestows reality on it. The object is real and interesting only insofar as it is impregnated by the subject:

> A man only is interested in anything when he identifies himself with it—he must himself be whirling and speeding through space like the

[36] Holloway, *op. cit.*, II, 63–76.
[37] Gita, 13.2.24.
[38] Notebook I, Holloway, *op. cit.*, II, 63–76.
[39] *Ibid.*

planet Mercury—he must be driving like a cloud—he must shine like the sun—he must be orbic and balanced in the air, like this earth—he must crawl like the pismire—he must—he would be growing fragrantly in the air, like the locust blossoms—he would rumble and crash like the thunder in the sky—he would spring like a cat on his prey—he would splash like a whale. . . .[40]

There is no doubt that Whitman's poetic fancy caught fire from astronomy and the celestial wonders that it revealed to his imagination. Whitman's interest in astronomy was aroused probably in the year 1847.[41] Astronomy opened out new inner horizons in the poet's mind and suggested the "transcendental" symbols appropriate to his inner growth and even aided that process. The ideas of cosmic flight, of space and time, which became in the "Song of Myself" symbols of the soul's dynamism, could have been suggested by the imaginary flights into the stellar spaces that Whitman had read about in astronomical literature. It is this sense of inner expansion suggested by astronomy that Whitman recorded in his notebooks.

All the vastness of Astronomy—and space—and systems of suns . . . carried in their computation to the farthest that figures are able . . . and then multiplied in geometrical progression ten thousand billion fold do not more than symbolize the reflection of the reflection, of the spark thrown off a spark, from some emanation of God. . . .[42]

and,

Afar in the sky was a nest,
And my soul flew thither and squat, and looked out
And saw the journeywork of suns and systems of suns. . . .[43]

Astronomical space and time suggest to him the notion of plenitude of being. Whitman speaks of the "Plenty of time and space."[44] And again, in a passage that describes the new mystical elation he had experienced, he says:

Amelioration is the blood that runs through the body of the universe—I do not lag—I do not hasten . . . I bide my hour over billions of years—

[40] *Ibid.*, p. 64.
[41] See Allen, *The Solitary Singer*, p. 123.
[42] Notebook II, Holloway, *op. cit.*, II, 86.
[43] *Ibid.*, p. 70.
[44] *Ibid.*

I exist in the . . . void that takes uncounted time and coheres to a nebula, and in further time cohering to an orb, marches gladly round, a beautiful tangible creature. . . . My right hand is time, and my left hand is space—both are ample—a few quintillions of cycles, a few sextillions of cubic leagues, are not of importance to me. . . .[45]

The same sense of timeless expansion is recorded in the following lines, which are among the first lines of Whitman's free verse: "I am alive in New York and San Francisco, / Again I tread the streets after two thousand years."[46]

As a result of this new birth Whitman now realizes the fulness and joy of being. He has overcome all the contractile elements of mind that characterized his "sick-soul" phase:

Poem incarnating the mind of an old man, whose life has been magnificently developed—the wildest and most exuberant joy—the utterance of hope and floods of anticipation—faith in whatever happens—but all enfolded in joy, joy, joy, which underlies and overtops the whole effusion.[47]

In this state of ecstasy he feels that life is a miracle, a "limitless and delicious wonder," and that body and soul, instead of being in conflict, are one.

My life is a miracle and my body which lives is a miracle; but of what I can nibble at the edges of the limitless and delicious wonder I know that I cannot separate them, and call one superior and the other inferior, any more than I can say my sight is greater than my eyes.[48]

In another remarkable notebook passage, in which musical, erotic, and astronomical images are mingled, Whitman describes how the ecstasy of physical sensation produced by listening to music causes in him a supreme sense of "dilation" and release, "uncaging" in him unsuspected powers.

I want the tenor, large and fresh as the creation, the orbed parting of whose mouth shall lift over my head the sluices of all the delight yet discovered for our race. I want the soprano that lithely overleaps the stars, and convulses me like the love-grips of her in whose arms I lay

[45] *Ibid.*, p. 79.
[46] *Ibid.*, p. 74.
[47] *Ibid.*, p. 79.
[48] *Ibid.*, p. 66.

last night. . . . I want the chanted Hymn whose tremendous sentiment shall uncage in my breast a thousand wide-winged strengths and unknown ardors and terrible ecstasies—putting me through the flights of all the passions—dilating me beyond time and air . . . calmly sailing me all day on a bright river with lazy slapping waves . . . and awakening me again to know by that comparison, the most positive wonder in the world, and that's what we call life.[49]

He also feels a certain largeness, a strange capaciousness within himself:

He drinks up quickly all terms, all languages and meanings. . . . To his curbless and bottomless powers, they be like ponds of rain water to the migrating herds of buffalo, who make the earth miles square look like a creeping spread.—See! he has only passed this way, and they are drained dry.[50]

There is also the urge for limitless expansion characteristic of the dynamic self:

I think the soul will never stop, or attain to any growth beyond which it shall not go.—When I walked at night by the sea shore and looked up at the countless stars, I asked of my soul whether it would be filled and satisfied when it should become God enfolding all these . . . and the answer was plain to me. . . . No, when I reach there, I shall want to go further still.[51]

Whitman has also known the transcendental character of the soul, its "greatness, immortality, purity."

"Never speak of the soul as anything but intrinsically great."[52] The only evil Whitman now seems to recognize is the metaphysical evil, namely, ignorance. Ignorance is bondage, wisdom release. He emphasizes the distinction between ignorance and wisdom, rather than that between good and evil. "The ignorant man is demented with the mania of owning things. . . . But the wisest soul knows that no object can really be owned."[53] The distinction between good and evil is a false distinction. The soul enfolds both good and evil. There is, in fact, no evil: "I am the poet of sin, / For I do not believe in sin."[54] Hence,

[49] *Ibid.*, p. 85.
[50] *Ibid.*, p. 84.
[51] *Ibid.*, p. 66.
[52] *Ibid.*, p. 53.
[53] *Ibid.*, p. 67.
[54] *Ibid.*, p. 71.

the all-inclusive soul encloses within itself the dualities of good and evil: "The universal and fluid soul impounds within itself not only all good characters and heroes, but the distorted characters, murderers, thieves." [55] The Gita makes out that the man of intelligence casts away both good and evil, for the perception of imperfection outside is an indication of imperfection within. And Whitman notes: "Wickedness is most likely the absence of freedom and health in the soul." And "The mean and bandaged spirit is perpetually dissatisfied with itself, and it is too wicked or too poor or too feeble." [56] The meditations of more than a decade and a half of spiritual life had now come to fruition. The poet of the *Leaves of Grass* was born. It now only remained for Whitman to give shape and expression to his thoughts. The years from 1848 to the appearance of the first *Leaves* represented the poet's struggle for self-expression, as the years preceding it marked the struggle for self-discovery. The inner conflicts and tensions of his early life were now at rest; Whitman had achieved inner peace. This sense of poise and self-possession which thus came of the liberating knowledge of the self did not leave him entirely, even in periods of crisis, and sustained him through much stress and turmoil.

# III

As Whitman came to realize that the secret of the universe was contained in his own self and that the highest wisdom was the effusion of the soul, he felt that his mission in life as a prophet and bard was "to articulate and faithfully express in literary or poetic form" [57] his own personality. True poetry is an autobiography of the soul. Goethe's "auto-biography" had earlier inspired in him a desire to write such a biographical work rendering the history of his soul's growth.[58] He was now resolved. "I will effuse egotism and show it underlying all, and I will be bard of personality." [59] This vast egotism in Whitman might have been, on a lower level, an abnormal narcissistic tendency rooted in his autoerotic emotions, but it certainly had an important

[55] *Ibid.*, p. 65–66.
[56] *Ibid.*, p. 65.
[57] "A Backward Glance," Holloway, *Complete Poetry and Selected Prose and Letters*, p. 860.
[58] See Holloway, *op. cit.*, I, 140.
[59] "Starting from Paumanok," 12.

role to play in his spiritual growth. It increased his mystical tendencies and turned him more and more upon himself. It developed in him, at an early period, the habit of communicating with his soul, while his strong homoerotic nature furnished the motive power for the enlargement of sympathies he was later to undergo.[60] As has been noted by scholars, Whitman's poetic personality was to him a powerful instrument for integrating his ego and overcoming original inhibitions and separation anxiety. *Leaves of Grass* was the outcome of a long process of sublimation.[61] His own egotism, moreover, brought him into a consciousness of the material objective universe, the not-me perpetually confronting the me, the mystical identity. He had known the English idealistic thinkers, Coleridge and Carlyle, and absorbed something, though perhaps indirectly, of the idealistic thought of Germany. It was finally, about 1847, when he discovered Emerson, that Whitman's vision attained clarity.

In his *Essays*, First (1841) and Second Series (1844), and in his *Addresses* (1836–38) Emerson, partly under the inspiration of the Hindu scriptures, to which he was early introduced through the Roy literature, developed a conception of self closely resembling the Hindu doctrine of *atman-brahman*. The central preaching of the essay "Self-Reliance" is "be thyself." It is only because man is weak and ignorant that he goes out of himself in search of support; he relies on objects, instruments, and the like. He looks for "foreign support," all the while forgetting his own "self-sufficiency" and "self-reliant soul." He is blind to the hidden pools of resources within himself. The reliance on outside objects is the want of self-reliance, the search for sufficiency outside one's self points to a deplorable sense of insufficiency within. So man ought to live "wholly from within." He should respect the laws of his own nature because his own law is the

----

[60] Havelock Ellis thinks that Whitman's inversion plays but a small part in his work. See *Studies in the Psychology of Sex* (Philadelphia: F. A. Davis, 1930), Vol. II (*Sexual Inversion*).

[61] See Gustav Bychowski, "Walt Whitman: A Study in Sublimation," *Psychoanalysis and the Social Sciences*, III, 223–61. Muriel Rukeyser says, "I venture to suggest that the inclusive personality which Whitman created from his own conflict is heroic proof of a life in which apparent antagonisms have been reconciled and purified into art" (*The Life of Poetry* [New York: Current Books, 1949], p. 78). That Whitman himself had been trying to understand his own egoistical nature during his formative period is indicated by the fact that he read a magazine article in 1845 on egotism (*Complete Writings*, Vol. VII, Part V, No. 219).

eternal law. The "inmost" and the "outmost" coincide in the self. Self-existence is the supreme end of life; for only thus can man conquer dualism and achieve "unity in nature and consciousness." In the hour of vision the soul perceives that the world of things, space, light, and time, is not diverse from itself; that the "aboriginal self" in man is the source of all life and all existence, "the foundation of action and of thought." This soul which is the prime mover and the underlying principle of things, is the "immense intelligence" [62] in which we all share. It is the one "universal mind," the "illimitable essence," the principle of identity running through the endless mutations of form. [63] In "Compensation" and "Over-soul" Emerson further develops the idea of a soul which is above the relational existence, of a transcendental self, the soul within man, the vast spiritual background and the substratum of all functions and states of consciousness. It is the self-luminous, self-effulgent light which illuminates the intellect and animates all organs and faculties. "The American Scholar" gives a mandate for knowing one's self. Emerson declares: "The world is nothing, the man is all; in yourself is the law of all nature ... in yourself slumbers the whole of Reason; it is for you to know all, it is for you to dare all." One cannot fail to see the striking resemblance between these ideas and the Upanishadic concept of *atman-brahman*. Ideas such as these no doubt helped Whitman gain the new consciousness. They formed the basis of his poetic thought. In this strong emphasis in Emerson's writings upon the soul Whitman could not have failed to recognize a close kinship to the deepest problems of his own nature, though, of course, in Whitman the personal and prophetic elements are to be rendered more conspicuous. This emphasis on the individual soul as the absolute reality belongs exclusively to Hindu mysticism.

It is your own self that is within all. That which breathes through the Prana, that which pervades through the Vyana, the self that inhabits the earth, the water, the fire, it is your own immortal self. The light that shines yonder is the light within you. The ultimate exists within your own self. That which is the subtle essence, that is the self, that is the true, and That Thou Art. [64]

[62] Cf., *Prajñānaghana*, "a mass of consciousness," Mandukya Upanishad, 5; *Vijñānamānandam Brahma*, "Brahman is knowledge and bliss," Brihadaranyaka Upanishad, 3.9.28.

[63] Emerson, "History."

[64] See Brihadaranyaka, 3.4.1, and Chhandogya, 6.5.2 and 6.8[.7].

If Whitman needed confirmation for his egocentric perspective, he could find it here in an ample measure, enough at any rate, to satisfy "the glut" of his soul. For Vedanta, better by far than any system in the West, effuses "egotism" and shows it "underlying all." The *atman*-centric way of Indian philosophy was a close analogy to Whitman's "animated ego style."[65]

*Leaves of Grass* was born out of a sense of fulness and completion in the poet. It was the expression of a full man and a completed process, the effusion of a soul that had come to itself. "I now thirty-seven years old in perfect health begin, / Hoping to cease not till death."[66] The poet had suddenly grown conscious of unsuspected depths in himself; what had long been maturing now reached fruition. In the exultation of the new discovery he shouts "eureka": "Whoever you are, to you endless announcements."[67] The new discovery that Whitman felt was the emergence of the transcendental self after a prolonged conflict and internal travail. Coming as it did, like a flash, this new sense left him in amazement. "This then is life," the poet exclaims: "Here is what has come to the surface after so many throes and convulsions."[68]

The new consciousness, which in the beginning arose as a passionate, though indistinct, yearning for immortality and a brooding sense of incompleteness and transience, resulted in an intensified spiritual activity and gradually grew into a deeper conviction in a permanent entity—the "soul" within himself. The sense of infinite existence became a realized fact, not a vain longing. This new conversion was marked by a "changed attitude of the ego"[69] and the emergence of a new set of values.

> I bring what you much need yet always have,
> Not money, amours, dress, eating, erudition, but as good,
> I send no agent or medium, offer no representative of value, but
> *offer the value itself.*[70]

Maya is the bondage to unreal values. Salvation is the passage into the realm of real values, from a small universe of petty desires into a larger

[65] *Complete Writings*, Vol. VII, Part III, No. 131.
[66] "Song of Myself," 1 (final version).
[67] "Starting from Paumanok," 14.
[68] *Ibid.*, 2.
[69] "the quite changed attitude of the ego": "A Backward Glance," Holloway, *op. cit.*, p. 861.
[70] "A Song for Occupations," 2. (Italics mine.)

spiritual life. "From the unreal lead me to the real, from darkness lead me to light, from death lead me to immortality"[71] is the prayer of the spirit craving for enlightenment. Men are outgoing in their tendencies and pursue objects of desire; they do not know their own world. It is only the discerning, whose intelligence is not engrossed by external objects, that set themselves to the task of finding "the eternal meanings."[72] The Katha Upanishad says: "The self-existent pierced the openings (of the senses) outward; therefore one looks outward, not within himself (*antarātman*). A certain wise man, while seeking immortality (*amṛtatvamichhan*) turned the eye inward and saw the self."[73] Whitman, the poet of the cosmos, advanced "through all interpositions and coverings and turmoils and stratagems to first principles."[74] It was by such an introspective vision, and a persistent effort not to be engrossed by the passing shows that Whitman was able to penetrate the veil of Maya and gain a knowledge of the essential self deep down within. To him, however, the inner vision and the outer are one and the same. Whether he is looking at the flowing panorama of life, or "meditating in some deep recess," he sees the same truth; beneath the surface of "qualities and things" he apprehends the essence. In intuitive knowledge introspection and extrospection coincide. For that which is outside is inside, that inside is outside. Hence do the Upanishads proclaim: "The self alone is to be meditated upon, the self alone should be realized, for one knows all this through it; this self is dearer than a son, dearer than wealth, dearer than everything else, and is innermost. One should meditate upon the self alone as dear."[75]

Beneath the flood of "ego" phantoms is the true self, the only real existence (*paramātman*). Hence "see the self and be the self" say the Vedantists. Whitman's own native tendencies led him to the exploration of his inner self; but it was, however, when he discovered Emerson that his thoughts were given a new drift and an added impetus. The vision of the true self dawned on him at first as a vague awareness of a certain doubleness or duality within himself. "I am always *conscious*

[71] Katha, 4.1, "*Asatō mā sat gamaya, tamasō mā jyōtirgamaya, mṛtyō mā amṛtam gamaya.*"
[72] "A Song for Occupations," 1.
[73] Katha, 4.1.
[74] Preface, 1855 Edition, Holloway, *op. cit.*, p. 581.
[75] Brihadaranyaka, 1.4.7–8.

*of myself as two*," he noted in his manuscript,[76] "as my soul and I," the "I" being the limited ego and "my soul" the universal soul. Spiritual knowledge starts with this self-awareness, this power to discriminate between the finite and the eternal, the apparent and the real. This idea of a permanent and universal self beneath the phenomenal folds is by no means peculiar to Whitman. The Hindu concept of self was gaining currency at the time by the popularization of the Hindu scriptures like the Gita, Vishnupurana, and the Upanishads; and all spiritually aspiring men, the Concordians especially, seem to have attempted to realize in their personal lives the truths which they had discovered in the Indian books. Curiously enough we come across similar utterances in Emerson and Thoreau, too. Emerson said in a speech in 1833:

> I recognize the distinction of the outer and the inner self; the *double consciousness* that within this erring, passionate, mortal self sits a supreme, calm immortal mind, whose powers I do not know; but it is stronger than I; it is wiser than I; it never approved me in any wrong; I seek counsel of it in my doubts; I repair to it in my dangers; I pray to it in my undertakings. It seems to me the face which the creator uncovers to his child.[77]

Thoreau wrote in *Walden*:

> I only know myself as a human entity; *the scene so to speak, of thoughts and affections*, and am *sensible of a certain doubleness* by which *I can stand as remote from myself as from another*. How intense my experience, I am conscious of the presence of and criticism of a part of me, which, as it were, is not a part of me, *but spectator, sharing no experience*, but taking note of it; and *that is no more I than it is you*. When the play of life is over, the spectator goes his way. It was a kind of fiction, a work of the imagination only, so far as he was concerned. . . .[78]

The idea of the self as the ground of all experience, and the spectator of the scene of the world, and the further conception that this self is the common self of all—is expressed here. Emerson speaks of the inner self or the immortal essence "within this erring, passionate, mortal self." The similarity between these ideas and the utterances of the Gita and the Upanishads is unmistakable; the Indian scriptures might have possibly been the sources for Emerson as well as Thoreau.

[76] Notebook 1, Holloway, *op. cit.*, II, 63–76. (Italics mine.)

[77] Quoted in Richard Garnette, *Life of Ralph Waldo Emerson* (London: Walter Scott Publishing Co., Ltd., 1888). (Italics mine.)

[78] Walden, chap. v, "Solitude." (Italics mine.)

In the case of Thoreau, it was undeniably so, for Thoreau read the "stupendous and cosmogonal philosophy of the Bhagwat Geeta"[79] during his Walden days and in his book quoted copiously from the Indian scriptures. The conception of the self, as a spectator unattached to actions and their consequences, and standing aloof from the world of events, is strikingly similar to the description of the sovereign self of the knower in the Bhagavad Gita.[80] For Whitman, too, the belief in the existence of a permanent self underlying all content of consciousness, a central identity persisting through all changes, is an unshakable conviction and forms the quintessence of his mystical realization. Whitman wrote in his notes, "He evidently thinks that behind all faculties of the human being, as the sight, the other senses and even the emotions and the intellect stands the real power, the *mystical identity the real I or Me or You.*"[81]

For him the ordinary condition of man is not his ultimate being; he has in him a deeper self. Emerson also expresses the same thought in the "Over-soul" essay. This unique conception that man's surface mentality does not constitute his real self, and that apart from and basic to the mind and its faculties is the spirit, which is the true self of man, and that this self is the universal self of all, is the fundamental thesis of Vedanta.[82] Whitman has, by means of his intuitive vision, penetrated to the spiritual center within himself and discovered the true glory and independence of his self. Early his intuition had led him to believe that his role in the world was more or less that of a detached witness. With the attainment of fuller realization he became convinced that his real self was different from the fettered ego that acts, enjoys, or suffers, that the outward events are not he, that his self is not a doer but a mere spectator, sharing all experience, yet unattached to it, standing apart and watching the masquerade of life:

> Trippers and askers surround me,
> People I meet, the effect upon me of my early life or the ward and
> city I live in, or the nation,

[79] *Ibid.*, chap xvi, "The Pond in Winter."

[80] The Self is no doer; work is done by the modes of nature, Gita, 3.27, 5.14, 13.29. The Self is the transcendental witness, subject and experiencer, 13.12.

[81] *Complete Writings*, Vol. VI, Part I, No. 28. (Italics mine.)

[82] See Mandukya Upanishad. The self is the *turiya* or "transcendental consciousness," the substratum of all other states of consciousness, the original unity beneath thought forms.

The latest dates, discoveries, inventions, societies, authors old and new,
My dinner, dress, associates, looks, compliments, dues,
The real or fancied indifference of some man or woman I love,
The sickness of one of my folks or of myself, or ill-doing or loss or lack
    of money, or depressions or exaltations,
Battles, the horrors of fratricidal war, the fever of doubtful news,
    the fitful events;
These come to me days and nights and go from me again,
*But they are not the Me myself.*

*Apart from the pulling and hauling stands what I am,*
Stands amused, *complacent*, compassionating, idle, unitary,
Looks down, is erect, or bends an arm on an impalpable certain rest,
Looking with side-curved head curious what will come next,
*Both in and out of the game and watching and wondering at it.*[83]

The self which says "they are not the Me myself," which witnesses
and waits while the endless spectacle of the world goes by, and which
retains its identity in the midst of the shifting processes is the transcendental witness in us, of which the scriptures speak. The poet who
wanders all night in his vision, dreaming all the dreams of the other
dreamers, who traverses the whole span of the universe, becoming by
turns the bride, the bridegroom, the hounded slave, and "the sleepless
widow looking out on the winter midnight" is the self as *sākṣi* or the
detached percipience.[84] The Upanishads describe two birds perching
on a tree, one of which feeds on the delicious fruit, while the other,
not tasting of it looks on.[85] The one is the empirical subject, the other
the perpetual percipient which sees but does not enjoy. The Gita
speaks of the supreme self in the body which is the witness, permitter,
supporter and the experiencer. "He appears to have the qualities of all
the senses, and yet is without the senses, *unattached* yet *supporting all,
free from the dispositions of Prakriti and yet enjoying them.*"[86] Though
participating in the world action this self is unfettered. According to
the Upanishads, "After enjoying himself and roaming, and merely

[83] "Song of Myself," 4. (Italics mine.)
[84] See Mahendranath Sircar, *Hindu Mysticism According to the Upanishads*
(London: Kegan Paul, French, Trubner & Co., Ltd., 1934), p. 282.
[85] Mundaka Upanishad, 3.1.1.
[86] Gita, 13.22; 13.14. (Italics mine.) Cf., "Both in and out of the game," "Song
of Myself," 4.

seeing good and evil, he [stays] in a state of profound sleep and comes back to his former condition. Whatever he sees there he is untouched by it, for this infinite being is unattached."[87] This consciousness of distinction between his real nature or "soul" and the phenomenal strata of his mind is constant in Whitman.

Critics have recognized a duplex personality in the *Leaves of Grass*,[88] an objective and a symbolic Whitman. Dr. Bucke considers this phenomenon to be common in men having cosmic consciousness.[89] This dual consciousness, as witnessed in Whitman, is not the pathological condition of the "divided self" that William James describes. James attributes this to a certain discordance or heterogeneity in the natural constitution of the subject. He cites the following case of Alphonse Daudet:

> Homo duplex, homo duplex! The first time that I perceived that I was two was at the death of my brother Henri, when my father cried out so dramatically: "He is dead, he is dead!" While my first self wept, my second self thought, "how truly given was that cry, how fine it would be at the theatre!" I was then fifteen years old.
>
> This horrible duality has often given me matter for reflection. Oh, this terrible second me, always seated whilst the other is on foot, acting, living, suffering, bestirring itself. This second me that I have never been able to intoxicate, to make shed tears, or put to sleep. And how it sees into things, and how it moves![90]

It is likely that this dual consciousness was brought home to Whitman's mind during crises of sensual ecstasies and sharpened by his habit of extricating himself from his own "experience." In some mysterious way, the very ecstasy of erotic sensation seems to release him from "anchors and holds," giving him a strange feeling of freedom and self-sufficiency. "What is it that frees me so in storms?" Through the

---

[87] Brihadaranyaka, 4.3.15; also Gita, 13.31–32. The supreme imperishable self neither acts, nor is tainted.

[88] See Clifton Joseph Furness, *Walt Whitman's Workshop* (Cambridge: Harvard University Press, 1928), n. 36, "Creative self as an identity separate from his ordinary self-conscious personality," "division of consciousness," "dual personality."

[89] *Cosmic Consciousness* (14th ed.; New York: E. P. Dutton & Co., 1948), p. 63.

[90] William James, *Varieties of Religious Experience* (New York: Modern Library, 1936), p. 164.

madness of erotic experience Whitman's "inebriate soul" rises supreme: "To rise thither with my inebriate soul!"[91]

This soul of Whitman is not a pose; nor is it his poetic faculty, that he in old age called "my Fancy," dramatized as a personality.[92] It is his transcendental self. When he says, "I believe in you my soul, the other I am must not abase itself to you / And you must not be abased to the other,"[93] the "soul" with which he communicates is the metaphysical essence, the cosmic consciousness, and the "other I am," the physical self or the ordinary consciousness. The "I" may be the grammatical subject of the speaker, strictly, indistinguishable from the physical self, but spoken of as a separate entity. Again, he thinks of himself as

> Another self, the *duplicate of everyone*, skulking and hiding it goes,
> Formless and wordless through the streets of the cities, polite and
>     bland in the parlors,
> In the cars of the railroads, in steamboats, in the public assembly,
> .  .  .  .  .  .  .  .  .  .  .  .
> . . . speaking not a syllable of itself,
> Speaking of any thing else but never of itself.[94]

This duplicate self is the perpetual witness in us. Through an assiduous practice of discrimination and by a persistent refusal to be deceived by appearances, Whitman has succeeded in getting at the essential soul in him, the noumenal entity in the center of phenomenal existence.

> Whoever you are, I fear you are walking the walks of dreams,
> I fear these *supposed realities* are to melt from under your feet and
>     hands,
> Even now your features, joys, speech, house, trade, manners, troubles,
>     follies, costume, crimes, dissipate away from you,

[91] "One Hour to Madness and Joy," in "Children of Adam." Also, "We Two, How Long We Were Fool'd," in "Children of Adam." Love acts as a liberating force and induces cosmic expansion.

[92] See Allen, *Walt Whitman Handbook* (New York: Hendricks House, Inc., 1957), p. 252, "Thus by being conscious of his imaginative faculty as a distinct identity or personality, which he addresses as 'my Soul' . . . he suceeds . . . in composing like 'one divinely possessed.' . . ." See also Gay Wilson Allen and Charles T. Davis, *Walt Whitman's Poems* (Grove Press, Inc., 1959), p. 11 (Introduction). Here Allen and Davis recognize that Whitman's "soul" in "Song of Myself" is not what he later called his Fancy—his poetic faculty.

[93] "Pioneers! O Pioneers!," in "Birds of Passage."

[94] "Song of the Open Road," 13. (Italics mine.)

Your true soul and body appear before me,
They stand forth out of affairs, out of commerce, shops, works, farms,
    clothes, the house, buying, selling, eating, drinking, suffering,
    dying.

.    .    .    .    .    .    .    .    .

O I could sing such grandeurs and glories about you!
*You have not known what you are, you have slumber'd* upon yourself
    all your life,
Your eyelids have been the same as closed most of the time,
*What you have done returns already in mockeries,*
(Your thrift, knowledge, prayers, if they do not return in mockeries,
    what is their return?)

*The mockeries are not you,*
Underneath them and within them I see you lurk,
I pursue you where no one else has pursued you,
Silence, the desk, the flippant expression, the night, the accustom'd
    routine, if these conceal you from others or from yourself, they
    do not conceal you from me,

.    .    .    .    .    .    .

The pert apparel, the deform'd attitude, drunkenness, greed, premature
    death, all *these I part aside.*[95]

Because of our false identification with the mind and the organs, we
mistake our real nature and think that "I am the body, I am these
organs," we feel as it were, think as it were, and move and shake as
it were, whereas our real self is far removed from such surface perturbations.[96] We hug shams and cherish illusions, "supposed realities."
But when through discriminate knowledge our wrong identification
is removed, all illusions melt and dissipate, and the "true soul"
emerges in its transcendent glory. "Where is he who tears off the
husks for you and me?" Whitman asks, "Where is he that undoes
stratagems and envelopes for you and me?"[97] It is only when, with
the aid of the discriminating intellect, one separates the outer coatings
of desires, passions, objects—superimposed on the self by ignorance,
that the kernel, the *ātman* is revealed. Only thus can one discover the
reality subsisting underneath the mockeries of affairs, commerce,
house, trades, joys, follies, etc. The poet strongly feels that it is the

[95] "To You," in "Birds of Passage." (Italics mine.)
[96] See Brihadaranyaka, 4.3.7 and 4.4.5–6, and Sankara's commentaries.
[97] "Song of the Open Road," 6.

self, finally, that survives the dissolution of material objects, the only immutable and identical substance amidst an outer region of change and impermanence.

> Quick sand years that whirl me I know not whither,
> Your schemes, politics, fail, lines give way, substances mock and elude me,
> Only the theme I sing, *the great and strong-possess'd soul eludes not,*
> *One's self must never give way—that is the final substance—that out of all is sure,*
> Out of politics, triumphs, battles, life, *what at last finally remains?*
> *When shows break up what but One's-self is sure?*[98]

To Whitman, the self alone is, in the ultimate analysis, reality; substances are elusive and unreal. The unseen soul governs absolutely at last.[99] The self is the substratum of the changing world of phenomena, which without such a world-ground would all be non-existent, mere apparitions. "The soul, its destinies, the *real real,* / (Purport of all these apparitions of the real)."[100] The Upanishads, too, express the same thought: "Now the designation for him is 'the Real of the Real' (*satyasya satyam*). Verily, breathing creatures are the real. He is their Real."[101] Again Whitman says,

> Thy body permanent,
> The body lurking there within thy body,
> The only purport of the form thou art, the real I myself,
> An image, an eidólon.[102]

The "real I myself" is the self lurking within; the outward form, the material shell, but an apparition. In "A Song for Occupations," Section 5, he declares that the only reality is the soul of persons, not things, and that "you and your soul enclose all things." It is also the self ultimately that confers value on the world and gives it its meaning

---

98 "Quicksand Years," in "Whispers of Heavenly Death." (Italics mine.)

99 "It was originally my intention after chanting in *Leaves of Grass* the songs of the body and existence, to . . . make the unseen soul govern absolutely at last" (Preface to the Centennial Edition, Holloway, *op. cit.*, p. 729).

100 "Thou Mother with Thy Equal Brood," 6. (Italics mine.) Also, "real of the real," "Riddle Song," in "From Noon to Starry Night."

101 Brihadaranyaka, 2.3.6.

102 "Eidólons," in "Inscriptions."

and vitality.[103] And this self, being the very root, is also the self of all.

This self is not, however, the dialectical being of the Germans, torn by an inner differentiation and caught in an endless web of relationships. It is suprarelational, indeterminate, and transcendental. It is completely independent of external laws, self-subsistent, and complete in itself. It is not the "many in one" of Hegel but an "identity," the soul identified with the infinite *brahman*,[104] the eternal self which remains immutable through the processes of metempsychosis. "To these proud laws of the air, the water and ground, *proving my interior soul impregnable*, / And nothing exterior shall ever take command of me."[105] This thought is very much the same as the Upanishadic conception of the self as the sovereign, the "lord of what has been and what is to be,"[106] as imperishable and unfettered, and transcending the relational existence. Again, the passage,

> *The soul is of itself,*
> All verges to it, all has reference to what ensues,
> All that a person does, says, thinks, is of consequence,[107]

has its source in the thought of Emerson: "There is a deeper fact in the soul than compensation, to wit its own nature. The soul is not a compensation, but a life. The soul is."[108] Whereas the world is governed by the laws of compensation, the soul is independent of such laws and subsists in its own right; "the soul is of itself"; it follows out its own laws and standards and is never the object of an external will. "Whatever satisfies souls is true;/ The soul has that measureless pride which revolts from every lesson but its own."[109] It is the lord of a "million

---

[103] See Preface to the Centennial Edition, Holloway, *op. cit.*, p. 734, "All serves, helps—but in the centre of all, absorbing all, giving for your purpose the only meaning and vitality to all, master and mistress of all, under the law, stands Yourself."

[104] The "identified soul" (Holloway, *op. cit.*, p. 693) is not the soul "that has received its identity"—the atomic individual; but it is the soul that has realized its potential divinity and universality, and attained selfhood. In other words, it is the self come to its own. Cf. Allen, *Walt Whitman Handbook*, pp. 303–11; Romain Rolland, *Prophets of New India: The Life of Vivekananda* (Almora: Advaita Ashram, 1944), p. 63.

[105] "Song of Joys." (Italics mine.)

[106] Katha, 4.5.

[107] "Song of Prudence," in "Autumn Rivulets." (Italics mine.)

[108] "Compensation."

[109] "Song of Prudence."

universes," bending them to its purposes, "All submit to them, where they sit, *inner, secure, unapproachable to analysis* in the soul."[110] Being pure and self-luminous, it effuses light out of itself. "Dazzling and tremendous how quick the sunrise would kill me / If I could not now and always *send sun-rise out of me*."[111] Being transcendental, it is unapproachable to ordinary imagination. "My final merit I refuse you, I refuse putting from me what I really am, / Encompass worlds, but never try to encompass me."[112]

> As if any man really knew aught of my life,
> Why even I myself I often think how little or nothing of my real life,
> Only a few hints, a few diffused faint clews and indirections
> I seek for my own use to trace out here.[113]

The real life of man is transcendental and eludes the grasp of the empirical mind. It is not possible for the biographer to give a real account of it. Only the soul in moments of insight can catch vaguest glimpses or faint echoes of the inner life. Whitman often feels that it is presumptuous of him to think that he has comprehended his real self, more so to have attempted to express it. It is this consciousness which sometimes gives rise to a sense of frustration in him:

> O baffled, balk'd, bent to the very earth,
> Oppress'd with myself that I have dared to open my mouth,
> Aware now that amid all that blab whose echoes recoil upon me, I have not once had the least idea who or what I am,
> But that before all my arrogant poems the real Me stands yet untouch'd, untold, altogether unreach'd.[114]

But it must not be supposed that to Whitman the self remained finally incomprehensible; for though it is transcendent to thought, it is not "unknowable," but is an experience, an immediate and immanent

[110] "Tests," in "Autumn Rivulets." (Italics mine.) Cf., Katha, 2.12, "ancient, hard to see, lodged in the inmost recess, located in intelligence."

[111] "Song of Myself," 25. (Italics mine.) Also, "of the inherent light greater than the rest," "Thoughts," in "From Noon to Starry Night." Cf. Brihadaranyaka, 4.3.6.

[112] "Song of Myself," 25.

[113] "When I Read the Book," in "Inscription."

[114] "As I Ebb'd with the Ocean of Life," 2, in "Sea-Drift."

reality. It is not an inference of the ratiocinating mind but an intuitive certainty.

> Facts, religions, improvements, politics, trades, are as real as before,
> *But the soul is also real, it too is positive and direct,*
> No reasoning, no proof has establish'd it.
> Undeniable growth has establish'd it.[115]

"Will you seek afar off?" asks Whitman, "you surely come back at last, / In things best known to you finding the best."[116] Again,

> It is not far, it is within reach,
> Perhaps you have been on it since you were born and did not know,
> Perhaps it is everywhere on water and on land.[117]

The quest of truth is not an outgoing journey but the realization of something implicit in the universe and the self. Only our eyes must be opened to the reality around us. Whitman declares this reality in "Starting from Paumanok" (13) and "A Song for Occupations" (2) "Was somebody asking to see the soul? / See your own shape and countenance, persons, substances, beasts, the trees, the running rivers, the rocks and sands." And "It is for you whoever you are, it is no farther from you than your hearing and sight are from you, / It is hinted by nearest, commonest, readiest, it is ever provoked by them." The Upanishads say, "The Brahman that is immediate and direct, the self that is within all."[118] Reality is known in every object, since it is the absolute core of things. It is not far off but immediate, *aparōkṣa*. So Whitman sings in "Song of Myself" (48), "I hear and behold god in every object." In the faces of men and women he sees god and finds letters from god dropped in the street. Reality to him is an enveloping presence. His mystical realization is not, however, as William James thinks[119] of a sporadic type; it is to him an ever present sense, governing his whole attitude and suffusing his outlook.[120]

---

[115] "A Song of the Rolling Earth," 3. (Italics mine.)

[116] "A Song for Occupations," 6.

[117] "Song of Myself," 46.

[118] Brihadaranyaka, 3.4.1, "*yat sākṣāt aparōkṣāt brahma ya ātmā sarvāntarah,*" and 3.7, "The immortal soul and the inner controller." Katha, 2.20, "in the heart of each living being."

[119] *Op. cit.,* p. 387.

[120] See Underhill, *op. cit.,* pp. 231–32, "Amongst modern men Walt Whitman possessed in a supreme degree the permanent sense of this glory."

From this supreme realization of self is born the mystic who has succeeded in integrating all the forces of his mind and achieved inner unity and peace. It is this knowledge of his true self that has enabled Whitman to shed all inhibitions and complexes and attain harmony and poise. For knowledge of the soul is immortality and strength. According to the Upanishad, with knowledge one wins immortality. The Kena (2.2) says, "The Brahman is known well, when it is known as the witness of every state of consciousness; for by such knowledge one attains immortality. *By this self he attains strength and by knowledge immortality.*" This knowledge came to Whitman. He is now no longer the sick soul torn by contrarieties and crying for light: "O Mystery of Death! I pant for the time when I shall solve you."[121] Now death presents no problem for him. He has realized the immortal essence in him, the eternal and the all-pervading. Immortality is now a certainty.

> I know I am deathless,
> I know this orbit of mine cannot be swept away by a carpenter's
>   compass,
> I know I shall not pass like a child's carlacue cut with a burnt stick
>   at night.[122]

Death is no longer an incubus weighing upon a stricken spirit but is a pathway to a higher and nobler existence; for Whitman has realized that so long as man is not freed from the bonds of material existence, the higher spiritual truths are not exhibited to him.[123] Whitman himself has been released by his spiritual knowledge from the bondage of matter, and has realized that his real self is an essence and its existence immaterial:

> The real life of my senses and flesh transcending my senses and flesh,
> My body done with materials, my sight done with material eyes,
> Proved to me this day beyond Cavil that it is not my material eyes
>   which finally see,
> Nor my material body which finally loves, walks, laughs, shouts,
>   embraces, procreates.[124]

Before this realization came to him, Whitman had been fighting his

[121] Holloway, *op. cit.*, II, 89.
[122] "Song of Myself," 20.
[123] See "Whispers of Heavenly Death."
[124] "A Song of Joys." See Chhandogya, 8.3.4, "after having risen from this body," and Sankara's commentary, "disembodied is the form of the self."

own tendencies, wrestling, so to say, with his own shadows. The evil
outside baffled him, and he saw much evil within. His spirit felt
cramped and bandaged in the coils of flesh; he felt the opposition of
matter. In "Nature" Emerson said, "The reason why the world lacks
unity, and lies broken and in heaps, is, because man is disunited with
himself." This might have been revealing to Whitman. The saying of
the Gita, "Let a man lift himself by himself; let him not degrade
himself; for the self alone is the friend of the self and the self alone is
the enemy of the self,"[125] is a theory of "self-reliance" par excellence.
Consequently, Whitman was led to search for unity within his own
self and found it there. He does not now feel any opposition, for all
sense of opposition is false. The world of material objects no longer
confronts him, for his own soul has become the soul of all beings.[126]
The opposition of the not-self has evaporated in the expansion of the
self. Whitman has arrived at the astounding conclusion, "Objects
gross and unseen soul are one."[127] Flesh is not evil; the conflict between
spirit and matter is an illusion. Even the sense of duality between body
and soul is false. Thus, he discovers, "Clear and sweet is my soul,
clear and sweet is all that is not my soul."[128] As a result of the attainment of the correct knowledge of self the false notion of the self as
opposed by a not-self is removed, and identity, is established. And
Whitman's question, "And if the body were not the soul, what is the
soul?"[129] is the result of his perception of identity, of a non-dualistic
conception of the universe.[130] This sense of the identity of body and
soul came to him with his new realization and was certainly not

[125] Gita, 6.5.
[126] Cf., "sarvabhūtātmabhūtātmā," Gita, 4.7.
[127] "A Song for Occupations," 5.
[128] "Song of Myself," 3. An extreme school of Vedantists do not recognize
the existence even of maya. See Gaudapada, Mandukya Karikas, Chapter 2.32,
"There is no dissolution, no birth, none in bondage, none aspiring for wisdom,
no seeker of liberation, and none liberated. This is the absolute truth". Even
according to Sankara, illusion or maya loses its reality the moment knowledge is
attained.
[129] "I Sing the Body Electric," 1, in "Children of Adam."
[130] See R. D. O'Leary, "Swift and Whitman as Exponents of Human Nature,"
*International Journal of Ethics*, Vol. XXIV. The view of the writer that "this
implied identification of body and soul represents a monistic conception of human
nature" supports this interpretation. To Whitman soul and body are one fact,
a single identity. Whitman does not recognize the merely animal and gross anywhere; all is spirit and all is divine.

present from the beginning.[131] Whitman's poems are exceptionally free from the spirit of dualism—of matter and spirit, subject and object, the sensible and the suprasensible—which is so prominent in Christian and Platonic mysticism.[132] Whitman, like the Vedantists, does not recognize the division of existence into the sensible and the suprasensible. The sensible resolves itself into the suprasensible, "the unseen is proved by the seen, / Till that becomes unseen and receives proof in its turn."[133]

From concrete life and materialism eventuate "invisible spiritual results" and the world of material objects is engulfed in the all-embracing self of the poet. In the self alone is real unity realized. When man comes to know that his own self is the infinite, universal *brahman*, all dualisms are ended, and all oppositions annulled. In the Upanishad, one sees that "The self alone is to be meditated upon, for all these are unified in it."[134] Real self-integration is possible only through the realization of the universal nature of the self. James's "heterogeneous personality" is the result of an inner schism, a dualism between the actual and the ideal, the ego and the universe. When the soul awakens to the perception of the ideal in the actual, and of the self in the all, equilibrium is achieved. It is thus that Whitman has been able to achieve what William James terms "healthy-mindedness," internal poise, and serenity of mind. Out of this supreme feeling of inward strength and fulness Whitman sings:

> Me imperturbe, standing at ease in Nature,
> Master of all or mistress of all, a-plomb in the midst of irrational
>     things,
> Me wherever my life is lived, O to be *self-balanced for* contingencies.[135]

We find this serene knowledge in "Song of Myself," 48: "I say to any man or woman, Let your soul stand cool and composed, before a million universes." Whitman has experienced "the joy of my soul leaning pois'd on itself."[136] His friends and critics testify to the extra-

[131] Note his early verse and manuscript jottings of the "journalistic" period, in which the sense of conflict is ever present.
[132] See Sircar, *op. cit.*, pp. 191–92.
[133] "Song of Myself," 3.
[134] Brihadaranyaka, 1.4.7.
[135] "Me Imperturbe," in "Inscriptions."
[136] "A Song of Joys."

ordinary equanimity and self-poise of the man. Edward Carpenter was struck by the absence in him of the fear of death and by the sense of eternal life in which he seemed always to live.[137] We have also Dr. Bucke's testimony:

> Perhaps, indeed, no man who ever lived liked so many things and disliked so few as Walt Whitman. . . . I never knew him to argue or dispute, and he never spoke about money. . . . He appeared to like all the men, women, children, he saw; he seldom expressed a preference for any person, . . . would not allow his tongue to give expression to fretfulness, antipathy, complaint, and remonstrance. He never spoke deprecatingly of any nationality or class of men, or time in the world's history, or against any trades or occupations—not even against any animals, insects, or inanimate things, nor any of the laws of nature, . . . such as illness, deformity, and death. He never complained or grumbled at the weather, pain, illness or anything else. . . . he never spoke in anger and apparently never was angry. *He never exhibited fear, and I do not believe he ever felt it.*[138]

Such a description of the character and mind of Whitman answers to the description of "Yogi" in the Gita as "free from dualities, firmly fixed in purity, possessed of the self," "even of mind," as one who neither loathes nor desires, who has ever the spirit of renunciation, who remains the same in pain and pleasure, who sees with an equal eye, who enjoys his peace from within, and who has conquered his self and attained the calm of self-mastery.[139]

For all his eager interest in the world Whitman was but a detached and passive witness. And through all its vagaries he possessed the same detachment and refused to become absorbed in the milieu of life. He describes himself as one who enjoys so much seeing the busy world move by him, and exhibiting itself for his amusement, while he takes it easy and observes.[140] Again, "After continued personal ambition and effort, as a young fellow to enter with the rest into competition for the usual rewards, business, literary, political, . . .

[137] See Edgar Lee Masters, *Whitman* (New York: Charles Scribner's Sons, 1937), p. 84.

[138] *Walt Whitman* (Philadelphia: David McKay, 1883), p. 221. See Isa, 7. With the perception of identity, all fear is expunged.

[139] Gita, 2.15, 2.45, 2.48, 3.18, 3.24, 4.3, 6.7.

[140] *Complete Writings*, Vol. V, Letters of 1868, Letter No. 5.

*I found myself remaining possessed."*[141] The eternal life is opened to Whitman; and he has now realized that the dualities of pain and pleasure, of fortune and misfortune obtain only in finite existence, while the infinite remains untouched. The truth of the great Upanishads has dawned on him: "The Infinite is bliss. There is no bliss in what is small. The Infinite alone is bliss. But one should understand the Infinite" (Chhandogya, 7.23.1). "The Self alone is immortal; everything else but him is mortal" (Brihadaranyaka, 3.7.23). "The Self is imperceptible for it is never perceived, undecaying for it never decays; unattached, for it is never attached; unfettered, it never feels pains, and never suffers injury" (Brihadaranyaka, 3.9.26). When Whitman understood this, he could sit and look out on the world of misery, evil, and suffering with supreme indifference and detachment. "All these— all the meanness and agony without end I sitting look out upon, / See, hear, and am silent."[142] Emperor Janaka said: "If Mithila is burnt, nothing that is mine is burnt." The *atman* is not tainted by the world's grief.[143]

> Over the mountain-growths disease and sorrow,
> An uncaught bird is ever hovering, hovering,
> High in the purer, happier air.[144]

The "uncaught bird" may be the poet's spirit which, though seated amidst miserable surroundings, stands aloof from them.[145] Knowledge exempts one from good and evil. The knower of the self transcends all ethical distinctions. "Apart from right, apart from the unright, / Apart from both what has been done and what has not been done" (Katha, 2.14). Consequently, Whitman has been freed from all sense of moral good and evil. "What blurt is this about virtue and about vice? / Evil propels me and reform of evil propels me, *I stand indifferent.*"[146]

[141] "A Backward Glance," Holloway, *op. cit.*, p. 860. (Italics mine.)
[142] "I Sit and Look Out," in "By the Roadside."
[143] See Katha, 5.11.
[144] "Song of the Universal," in "Birds of Passage." The optimism expressed in this poem might seem to be of the Hegelian type. Whitman derived much solace from Hegel's philosophy of harmonious becoming in his later days when the disturbing national tragedy of the Civil War and the darkening social outlook had considerably shaken his faith in America's manifest destiny.
[145] See Katha, 2.12, "Seated amidst miserable surroundings the intelligent man renounces joy and grief."
[146] "Song of Myself," 22.

The presence of contradictions in the world does not disturb his composure.

> Do I contradict myself?
> Very well, then, I contradict myself;
> (I am large—I contain multitudes).[147]

For Whitman has realized the self, the principle of identity underlying all contradictions. Diversities are embraced in the consciousness of oneness; contradictions are finally lost in the identity of the self.

William James has noticed in Whitman "an inability to feel evil"—a tendency he calls "healthy-mindedness." Whitman's optimism is not, however, a facile quality of mind, nor bravado, nor a kind of cannibalism. It is but the natural concomitant of his attainment of metaphysical knowledge, the result of the conviction that evil is an unreality, to be sloughed off, outgrown, and negated. Evil is a lie; it simply does not arise when the soul awakens to its real being. Healthy-mindedness follows on overcoming dualities. Whitman, among modern men, is an outstanding example of such a condition of perfect freedom from dualities. Carlyle, despite his earnestness, remained a "sick-soul," haunted by the spectre of world-destruction.[148] Emerson suffered from congenital low spirits. "I shiver in and out." "My pulse is slow, my blood is cold, my stammering tongue is rudely turned." Emerson lacked the fulness of spirit that Whitman possessed. There was a sickliness and a want of vitality about him. Neither could Emerson achieve the perfect internal harmony that Whitman did. There was still a discord, a duality, lurking in Emerson's personality. He was inhibited by his inherent puritanism. His journals are confessions of this conflict; in him much remained unrealized.[149] Thoreau, too, could not, in spite of his remarkable peace and poise, rise to Whitman's attitude of unqualified approval and universal affirmation. He was a man of denials, as Whitman was a man of affirmations.[150]

---

[147] *Ibid.*, 51.

[148] See "Carlyle from American Points of View," Holloway, *op. cit.*, p. 785.

[149] See Holbrook Jackson, *Dreamers of Dreams* (London: Faber & Faber, Ltd., 1948), Chapter on Emerson.

[150] *Ibid.*, p. 256, "Leaves of Grass is a fanfare of affirmations ... Whitman is Nature's 'yes' man, the personification of the Everlasting Yea." *Walden* is full of criticisms and negations. Contrast Whitman, "My gait is no fault-finder's or rejector's gait," "Song of Myself," 22.

Such faith in the supremacy of self could not be shaken from Whitman's mind. Through poverty, degradations, and conflicts, Whitman held his conviction that his real self would come forth triumphant, overmastering all.[151] Critics have expressed the view that the 1860 edition records a spiritual crisis in Whitman's life and that the poet was troubled by some deep perturbations of sexual passion. According to this view, the "Calamus" cluster and poems like "As I Ebb'd with the Ocean of Life" and "Out of the Cradle Endlessly Rocking" reflect such a crisis.[152] However, the fateful character of the "Calamus" love is only apparent, for, the saving knowledge of self never deserted Whitman even in his moments of deepest perturbation,[153] and it sustained him through all struggles and turmoils of life. The supreme spirit of detachment and renunciation is preserved in the midst of the deepest passions:

> Whoever you are holding me now in hand,
> Without one thing all will be useless,
> I give you fair warning before you attempt me further,
> *I am not what you supposed, but far different.*
>
> .    .    .    .    .    .    .    .
>
> But these leaves conning you con at peril,
> For these leaves and me you will not understand,
> They will elude you at first and still more afterward,
> *I will certainly elude you.*
>
> .    .    .    .    .    .
>
> For all is useless without that which you may guess at many times and
>          not hit, that which I hinted at;
> Therefore *release me and depart on your way.*[154]

And elsewhere, "What beckonings of love you receive you shall only answer with passionate kisses of parting,/ You shall not allow the hold of those who spread their reach'd hands towards you."[155] Whitman,

---

[151] "Ah, Poverties, Wincings," in "From Noon to Starry Night".

[152] See Allen, *Walt Whitman Handbook*, pp. 68, 87, 145. Also, *The Solitary Singer*, chap. vi.

[153] See Holloway, *op. cit.*, II, 94, Notebook 9 (dated 1868–70). Perhaps inspired by Epictetus, Whitman noted down the following self-instruction: "It is imperative that I obviate and remove myself (& my orbit) at all hazards ... from this incessant & enormous ... Perturbation."

[154] "Whoever You Are Holding Me Now in Hand," in "Calamus." (Italics mine.)

[155] "Song of the Open Road," 11.

the impassioned lover of comrades, is all the while escaping the bonds of his affections. Each confession of love is followed by a clear recognition that he is untouched by his passions, and each time his comrade is warned that "I am not what you supposed, but far different," that he cannot be entangled in his love because his real self is elusive.[156] Whitman recognizes the binding quality of love and resists strongly the tendency to be enslaved by it. The spirit of inward withdrawal and renunciation never leaves him for a moment. In the office or on the battlefront, nursing in the hospitals or lying ill in bed, the consciousness that "they are not the Me myself" is never absent from his mind.

As a result of this self-realization and the consequent expulsion of all contrary elements, Whitman feels an ineffable sense of fruition and fulness. "I am satisfied, I see, dance, laugh, sing."[157] Eternity is blissful being; it is the state of self-fulfilment. The mystic who has found the supreme self feels no urges and is disturbed by no desires, for the self is eternally realized. The knower of the self is once for all freed from the endless processes of becoming. It is this supreme state that is indicated in the following lines:

> I exist as I am, that is enough,
> If no other in the world be aware I sit content,
> And if each and all be aware I sit content.[158]

The Upanishads point out that the man of realization lives in the peace that comes of self-fulfilment. He attains all the objects of desire, since they are but the self to him. To realize the self (*ātmakāma*) is to have all desires satisfied (*āptakāma*) and thus to transcend desires (*akāma*).[159] Dissatisfaction is symptomatic of the "bandaged spirit." The poet has vowed to himself: "Wherever I have been I have charged myself with contentment and triumph."[160] The animals bring him tokens of his own attitude. "They do not sweat and whine." Not one is dissatisfied.[161] One's world is nothing but one's own self; he who has gained his self gains the whole world. The Brihadaranyaka (1.4.15) tells us: "One should meditate only upon the world called the

156 "Even as a lotus leaf is untouched by water," Gita, 5.10.
157 "Song of Myself," 3.
158 *Ibid.*, 20.
159 Brihadaranyaka, 1.3.21.
160 "Thoughts," in "Songs of Parting."
161 "Song of Myself," 32.

Self," and Whitman echoes, "One world is aware and by far the largest to me, and that is myself."[162] The self alone is one's greatest wealth and glory, one's supremest world and bliss.[163] One who has experienced one's self-sufficiency need not look for wealth outside one's self.

> Henceforth I ask not good-fortune, *I myself am good-fortune,*
> Henceforth I whimper no more, *postpone no more, need nothing,*
> Done with indoor complaints, libraries, querulous criticisms,
> *Strong and content* I travel the open road.[164]

The soul alone will maintain itself: "I will make the *true poem of riches* | To earn for the body and the mind whatever adheres and goes forward, and is not dropt by death."[165] The true poem of riches is the "Song of Myself." The scriptures describe the wise man who has attained his self as one who has delight in the self (*ātmaratih*), who revels with the self (*ātmacrīdah*), who is content with the self (*ātmanyēvaca santustah*), who has intercourse with the self (*ātmamithunah*), and who has bliss in the self (*ātmānandah*). Such a man becomes autonomous (*svarāt* or self-king).[166] Whitman, too, has attained to his soul's natural and supreme state. He knows he is "august," and he is content to live in the ecstasy of self-communion: "O soul thou pleasest me, I thee."[167] With this sovereignty he can declare, "I dote on myself, there is that lot of me and all so luscious. | *Each moment and whatever happens thrills me with joy.*"[168]

His habit of entering into a mystical intercourse with his soul, which induces in him an ecstatic, even erotic, feeling—finds a notable expression here:

> I believe in you my soul. . . .
>
> .　.　.　.　.　.　.
>
> Loafe with me on the grass, loose the stop from your throat,

[162] "Song of Myself," 3. .
[163] Brihadaranyaka, 4.3.32, "*ēṣa'sya paramā gatih, eṣa'sya paramā sampat, ēṣō'sya paramō lōkah, eṣō'sya paramānandah.*"
[164] "Song of the Open Road," 1. (Italics mine.)
[165] "Starting from Paumanok," 12. Also, "The most affluent man is he that confronts all the shows he sees by equivalence out of the stronger wealth of himself" (Holloway, *op. cit.*, p. 578).
[166] See Chhandogya, 7.25.1; Gita, 3.17.
[167] "Passage to India," 8.
[168] "Song of Myself," 24. (Italics mine.)

Not words, not music or rhyme I want, not custom or lecture, not
even the best,
Only the lull I like, the hum of your valvèd voice,
I mind how once we lay such a transparent summer morning,
How you settled your head athwart my hips and gently turn'd over
upon me,
And parted the shirt from my bosom-bone, and plunged your tongue,
to my bare-stript heart,
And reach'd till you felt my beard, and reach'd till you held my feet.[169]

It is through this feeling of fulfilment that Whitman has gained the
sense of eternal "being," the eternal "now" of the mystic. "This
minute that comes to me over the past decillions, / There is no better
than it and now."[170] The realized self is not a growth or becoming
but a fulfilment and being. A life of ever increasing aspiration is
inconsistent with self-knowledge. It is thus that Whitman arrives at
the conclusion that the real is perfect and ideal, and that nothing can
improve upon the goodness and completeness of his present existence.
In "A Song for Occupations," 6, he tells us, "Happiness, knowledge,
not in another place but this place, not for another hour but this hour."
Perfection is not to be sought as a distant ideal but is to be known as
already accomplished in the actual and the now. It is this sense that is
suggested in these words of Thoreau:

Men esteem truth remote, in the outskirts of the system, behind the
farthest star, before Adam and after the last man. In eternity there is
indeed something true and sublime. But all these times and places and
occasions are now and here. God himself culminates in the present
moment, will never be more divine in the lapse of all the ages.[171]

[169] *Ibid.*, 5.
[170] *Ibid.*, 22.
[171] *Walden*, chap. iii.

# CHAPTER FOUR

# The Dynamic Self

"And thee my soul,
Joys, ceaseless exercises, exaltations"
("Eidólons," in "Inscriptions")

When Whitman had achieved this attenuation of ignorance and the realization of the true glory of the self, there was an immense widening of the inner horizon. The process of growth into the larger self was one of expansion and enlargement. With the release from all flexions and constraining elements, the self became fluid and entered into all.[1] This supreme sense of liberation, or *mōksa*, the awakening from false self-limitations, finds utterance in a memorable passage of the Mundaka Upanishad (2.2.8): "When he that is both high and low is seen, the knot of the heart is loosened, all doubts are dissipated; and all his *karma* is consumed."

> From this hour I ordain myself *loos'd of limits and imaginary lines,*
> *Going where I list,* my own master total and absolute,
>
> .    .    .    .    .    .    .    .    .    .
>
> Gently, but with undeniable will divesting myself of the holds that
>    hold me.[2]

Since self-knowledge is the knowledge of the identity of the individual and the universal self, it results in universal identification. "When he imagines that he is a god, that he is a king, and that 'I am this world— all,' that is his highest state," according to the Upanishad.[3] The self that realizes its own sufficiency and glory begins a career of infinite expansion, and the world of objects is the creation of its expansive activity. From self-knowledge proceeds all creative activity. The Brahman knew only himself as "I am Brahman" and he became all; the creation is his self-projection. The same with men and sages.

---

[1] See Prasna Upanishad, 4.11, *sarvamēvāviśēti.*
[2] "Song of the Open Road," 5. (Italics mine.)
[3] Brihadaranyaka, 4.3.20.

Whoever knows this becomes all that. The sage Vamadeva, while realizing his own self as identical with That, began to feel that he was Manu and the sun.[4] Following on self-knowledge comes the consciousness that "I am all." Since identification or expansion is a centrifugal movement, it gives rise to an internal dynamism; limitless pools of energy are released from within, and they find an outlet in creative activity. This phase marks the return of the spirit from its inner recesses into the world of dynamic activity, even as it is inevitably followed by a return back to itself—withdrawal and self-immersion.

Whitman the cosmic poet is the creative phase of the self; *Leaves of Grass* is the embodiment. The work has grown out of an irresistible impulse, the cosmic urge for creation. The poet and the book are identical. "Camerado, this is no book, / Who touches this touches a man."[5] The work is an outcropping of the poet's personality, the emanation of his vital, dynamic self.

As a result of this self-knowledge, the poet has become conscious of tremendous powers within himself. With the overcoming of all bonds and inhibitions and the consequent enlargement of consciousness there is a tremendous flow of vital energy which manifests itself in an immense exuberance of spirit and self-assertion. The sage who sounds his "barbaric yawp over the roofs of the world" declaring himself "infinite and omnigenous," is at once the greatest prophet and creator. With this magnification the poet realizes that he is a god and creator: "The supernatural of no account, myself waiting my time to be one of the supremes. / . . . *becoming already a creator.*"[6] He does not shrink before the gods: he matches them. He outbids Hercules and takes on the exact dimensions of Jehovah. And he is the cosmic creator projecting the history of the future.[7] This creative activity of the self is described in the following lines of the Upanishad:

> There are no chariots there, no spans, no roads.
> But he projects from himself chariots, spans, roads.
> There are no blisses there, no pleasures, no delights.
> But he projects from himself blisses, pleasures, delights. For he is a creator.[8]

[4] *Ibid.*, 1.4.10.
[5] "So Long," in "Songs of Parting."
[6] "Song of Myself," 41. (Italics mine.)
[7] "To a Historian," in "Inscriptions."
[8] Brihadaranyaka, 4.3.10.

In his expansive activity Whitman feels he is limitless; he is not contained between his hat and boots. He feels in himself a superabundance of energy. "I permit to speak at every hazard. / Nature without check with original energy."[9] The "Spontaneous Me" and "barbaric yawp" of Whitman—which so disturbed Santayana—are but a natural expression of the dynamic self, directly consequent on its dynamic expansion.

> . . . I have stores plenty and to spare,
> And any thing I have I bestow.
>
> .        .        .        .        .        .
>
> I seize the descending man and raise him with resistless will,
> O despairer, here is my neck,
> By God, you shall not go down! hang your whole weight upon me.[10]

Spontaneous creation and unrestricted movement characterize this state of release. When the self attains liberation and is lifted into the largeness of spirit, "he becomes lord himself, his movements are unfettered in all the worlds" (*kāmacāri*).[11] Consequently, Whitman says, "Going where I list, my own master total and absolute." There is an expansion of inner dimensions: "What widens within you Walt Whitman? / Within me latitude widens, longitude lengthens."[12] The same expansive vision, and the feeling of liberation are expressed in "A Song of Joys," "O joy of my spirit—it is uncaged—it darts like lightning." And we see elsewhere:

> Space and Time! now I see it is true, what I guess'd at,
> What I guess'd when I loaf'd on the grass,
>
> .        .        .        .        .        .
>
> My ties and ballasts leave me, my elbows rest in sea-gaps,
> I skirt sierras, my palms cover continents,
> I am afoot with my vision.[13]

When the self is realeased from the narrow bonds of the finite

---

[9] "Song of Myself," 1.
[10] *Ibid.*, 40.
[11] Chhandogya, 7.25.2.
[12] "Salut au Monde," 1–2.
[13] "Song of Myself," 33.

material world, it also escapes the bondage of time and space—the ordinary psychological entities—and enters the realm of "spiritual time and space."[14] The dynamic being sees time and space as symbols of its dynamism. Space is expanse, and time is creativity and emergence. The spirit becomes so greedy that it wants to embrace all time and all space; "All space, all time" Whitman calls in "Eidó'lons." And in "A Song of Joys" he claims, "It is not enough to have this globe or a certain time. I will have thousands of globes and all times." As the consciousness expands, the soul becomes a *kāmacāri*, "going where I list," and a disembodied spirit:

> Speeding through space, speeding through heaven and the stars,
> Speeding amid the seven satellites and the broad ring, and the diameter
>     of eighty thousand miles,
> .     .     .     .     .     .     .     .     .
> Storming, enjoying, planning, loving, cautioning,
> Backing and filling, appearing and disappearing,
> I tread day and night such roads.[15]

In its flight across the worlds the soul feels no obstacles; nothing can impede its course. It has access to "material and immaterial." The "fluid and swallowing soul" departs as air, and shakes its white locks at the runaway sun.[16] As the barriers that bound him are broken and the holds that would hold him are loosed, he enjoys ease and release from the oppressive divisions of discrete time and place. The differences of place, distant and near, of past, present, and future are merged into a living sense of the present, and the essence of existence is felt everywhere the same. Time and space are seen as a vast spiritual expanse, a flow or continuum. We find such expansiveness echoed again and again: "Distant and dead resuscitate, / They show as the dial or move as the hands of me, I am the clock myself," and, "It avails not, time or place—distance avails not, / I am with you, you men and women of a

---

[14] See Mahendranath Sircar, *Hindu Mysticism: According to the Upanishads* (London: Kegan Paul, French, Trubner & Co., Ltd., 1934), p. 301.

[15] "Song of Myself," 33. See also "Song of the Open Road," 5, and Emory Holloway, *Uncollected Poetry and Prose* (New York: Doubleday, Doran, & Co., 1922), II, 79–80; "Infinitude the flight: fathomless the mystery. Man so diminutive dilates beyond the sensible universe, competes with, outcopes space and time," in "Democratic Vistas." *Complete Poetry and Selected Prose and Letters*, edited by Emory Holloway (London: Nonesuch Press, 1938), p. 714.

[16] "Song of Myself," 52.

generation, or ever so many generations hence." and, "I am alive in New York and San Francisco, / Again I tread the streets after two thousand years."[17] This sense of continuity may be seen in these words of Jallaluddin Rumi, the Persian mystic:

> Eve was not, I was
> Adam was not, I was
> He himself was not, I was.

The process of self-opening now complete, Whitman feels that he is identical with the universal movement outside. The cosmic being outside and the vivifying self within are realized as one and the same. For he who knows his "actual self"—the reality beneath his empirical being—knows himself to be the permeating essence of the cosmic existence outside, because his own self is the self of all, "every atom belonging to me as good belongs to you." Thus, Whitman comes to feel that he is himself the cosmic whole. He describes himself as "Walt Whitman, a Kosmos." He is "self-conscious microcosmic."[18] He will contain everything, even contradictions, within himself. He is "of old and young, of the foolish as much as of the wise, . . . stuff'd with the stuff that is coarse, and stuffed with the stuff that is fine, . . . the smallest the same, the largest the same,"

> Of every hue and caste am I, of every rank and religion,
> A farmer, mechanic, artist, gentleman, sailor, quaker,
> Prisoner, fancy-man, rowdy, lawyer, physician, priest.[19]

and realizing this, he realizes the opposite as well, for he sees that " *The universe is in myself—it shall pass through me as a procession.*"[20] The liberated self feels his oneness so intensely that he, like Emerson's "Brahma," calls himself a creator—all-pervading: "I am the food, I am the food-eater; I am the subject, I am the object; I am the two together; I am the first-born, the destroyer of the world also. I am the

---

[17] *Ibid.*, 33; "Crossing Brooklyn Ferry," 3; Holloway, *op. cit.*, II, 74.

[18] "Walt Whitman, the sturdy, self-conscious microcosmic, prose-poetical author of that incongruous hash of mud and gold—*Leaves of Grass*," in "Street Yarn." Holloway, *op. cit.*, p. 604.

[19] "Song of Myself," 16.

[20] *Complete Writings of Walt Whitman* (New York: G. P. Putnam's Sons, 1902), Vol. VI, Part I, No. 49.

sun-like light. I am the centre of the world, of immortal gods."[21]
"He sees all things, becomes all things; though one it becomes
threefold, fivefold, sevenfold, ninefold, twenty, hundred, thousand-
fold."[22] In its terrific expansive activity the soul sweeps the skies and
outruns the globes: "I, indeed, am below, I am above. I am to the west.
I am to the east. I am to the south. I am to the north. I, indeed, am this
whole world."[23] Whitman too, like the *viśwarūpa* or cosmic form,[24]
includes diversity and "resists anything better than my own diversity."[25] Like the cosmic Krishna of the Gita, who is but a poetic
representation of the expanded self of the mystic, he says, "I am the
actor, the actress, the voter, the politician, / The emigrant and the
exile, the criminal that stood in the box."[26]

And so he sees himself in all people and identifies himself with the
sorrows of the world;[27] he is as much good as evil; he interpenetrates
all life and existence. Thus, "Chanting the Square Deific" is not
simply a dramatization of the fourfold character of the divine idea,
but a mystic utterance of the self that has identified with cosmic
manifold and sees itself as its creator, including within itself the whole
cosmos, with all its aspects of justice, law, benevolence, and the like.
Whitman's soul is the "general soul," the center and essence of the
universe. Concomitantly, following on this cosmic expansive consciousness is the power of prophecy or cosmic insight. When man
rises above the purely subjective level to the cosmic, his thoughts will
coincide with the thoughts of the world. One's real self is the cosmic
self, and, knowing it, one knows all; one thinks cosmically and feels
cosmically. This is the meaning of the Upanishadic saying: "Of all
these, the self alone is to be realized, for one knows all these through
it."[28] The deeper consciousness of man is one with the universal mind.

---

[21] Taittiriya, 3.10.6.

[22] Chhandogya, 7.26.2.

[23] *Ibid.*, 7.25.1.

[24] See Gita, 11.

[25] "Song of Myself," 16.

[26] "The Sleepers," 1; cf. Gita, 9.16, 19, 29, "I am the ritual action, I am the sacrifice, I am the hymn, also the melted butter; I am immortality and also death, I am
being as well as non-being."

[27] "Ramakrishna howled with pain when he saw two boatmen quarreling.
He came to identify himself with the sorrows of the whole world. . . ." Romain
Rolland, *The Life of Ramakrishna* (New York: Albert & Charles Boni, 1930),
p. 83.

[28] Brihadaranyaka, 1.4.7.

To one who has reached it nothing is hidden or unknown. One becomes omniscient. It is thus that Whitman declares;

> These are really the thoughts of all men in all ages and lands, they are not original with me,
> If they are not yours as much as mine they are nothing or next to nothing,
> If they are not the riddle and the untying of the riddle they are nothing,
> If they are not just as close as they are distant they are nothing.[29]

Prophecy is not prediction merely; it is cosmic intuition or the power of apprehending and revealing the truths implicit in the universe.

Consistent with his dynamism and fulness of being, the ideas of expansion, fecundity, and plenitude dominate Whitman's poetry and thought. To a certain extent, no doubt, these ideas were typically American and nationalistic.[30] In a very genuine sense Whitman's dynamism is the product and expression of a dynamic age. The fulness of expanding America facilitated the inner expansion of his soul, and the abundance of the natural life amidst which Whitman was born and brought up contributed to the growth of his spirit by imparting to him freshness and an exuberant vigor. The dauntless pioneering of the American land made for pioneering and discovery in the realm of spirit. Consequently, the ideas of expansion and dynamism permeate his thought; the poet reads everywhere symbols of his dynamic spirit. The sea, which captured his imagination and always remained an "invisible influence"[31] in his poetry, is a symbol of dynamism.

> In cabin'd ships at sea,
> The boundless blue on every side expanding.
>
> .   .   .   .   .   .   .   .   .   .   .
>
> *We feel the long pulsation, ebb and flow of endless motion.*
> *The tones of unseen mystery, the vague and vast suggestions, of the briny*
>    *world the liquid-flowing syllables,*
>
> .   .   .   .   .   .   .   .   .   .   .

[29] "Song of Myself," 17.

[30] See Gay Wilson Allen, *Walt Whitman Handbook* (New York: Hendrick House, Inc., 1957), p. 284.

[31] "Afterward, I recollect, how it came to me that instead of any special lyrical or epical or literary attempt, the sea-shore should be an invisible *influence*, a pervading gauge and tally for me...." "Sea-Shore Fancies," Holloway, *op. cit.*, p. 738.

*The boundless vista and the horizon far and dim are all here,*
*And this is ocean's poem.*[32]

The sea symbolizes motion, mystery, and immensity. In the endless pulsation of the sea the poet discovers a close kinship to his own dynamic, vitalistic self. In its boundless vistas and its far and dim horizon, he reads tokens of his own ever opening spiritual expanse. The ship sailing the "boundless blue" suggests his own adventurous and exploring soul launching out into the unknown. Likewise, astronomy, with its discoveries of infinite universes and vast expanses of space, provides a boundless field for Whitman's expanding self. In the "ever-darting globe, through Space and Air,"[33] and in the ceaseless spinning of the constellations,[34] the mystic finds close analogies to his inner dynamism. "Wider, wider they spread, expanding, always expanding, / Outward and outward and forever outward."[35]

By matching his spirit against the orbs, he measures his own magnitude. Whitman values science at all for the great expansion it has effected in the realm of thought by opening up new universes to human ken, new vistas and possibilities.[36] Whitman's conception of poetry, too, is pre-eminently dynamic. Poetry must be "all-surrounding and Kosmical."[37] In "A Backward Glance" Whitman declares: "It is almost as if a poetry with cosmic and dynamic features of magnitude and limitlessness suitable to the human soul, were never possible before."[38] But he also warns, "The largeness of the nation, however, were monstrous without a corresponding largeness and generosity of the spirit of the citizen."[39] Whitman insists that the fulness of nature should lead to a corresponding fulness of spirit. And the cosmic poet should incarnate the largeness and fecundity of nature, of his geography and national life, and that poetry should be commensurate with the magnitude of the human soul, which it seeks to express, and equal to its needs. True art, according to him, should be the organ of the dynamic self. Literature should vocalize the dynamics of the soul and prove

[32] "In Cabin'd Ships at Sea," in "Inscriptions."
[33] "A Voice from Death," in "Good-Bye My Fancy."
[34] "Fancies at Navesink," in "Sands at Seventy."
[35] "Song of Myself," 45.
[36] See Holloway, *op. cit.*, p. 734.
[37] "Democratic Vistas," Holloway, *op. cit.*, p. 708.
[38] *Ibid.*, p. 863.
[39] *Ibid.*, p. 572, Preface, 1855 Edition.

equal to the demands of an expansive consciousness.[40] Whitman's verse, too, breathes the spirit of inward freedom and release; it is as free from poetic convention as his life was from social convention. Free verse is the only proper vehicle of a poetry of energy.[41] Likewise, his dynamic self feels restive under the staticness of the old world and its stagnant spirit. Custom, convention, and conformity are all crusts that flatten the spirit. The world's problem, Whitman feels, is that it is rigid and lacks fluidity. "Our country seems to be threatened," Whitman wrote, "with a sort of ossification of the spirit."[42] Similarly, in "Fecund America" Whitman sees the fulness and plenitude of his own being:

> Loud O my throat, and clear O soul!
> The season of thanks and the voice of full-yielding
> The chant of joy and power for boundless fertility.[43]

*Leaves of Grass* was thus created out of an inner sense of profundity and fulness. It is the expression of a highly developed consciousness in the poet who, by dint of his superior knowledge, has succeeded in remaking his whole nature and achieved internal harmony and poise of being. The work was born as the necessary self-expression of the dynamic spirit, rather than as a compensation for failures in the outer world of reality.[44] For instead of seeking an adjustment to the world of practical aspirations, Whitman came to view it in a new light, and with

[40] "While, current and novel, the grandest events and revolutions, and stormiest passions of history, are crossing today with unparallel'd rapidity and magnificence over the stages of our own and all the continents, offering new materials, opening new vistas, with largest needs, inviting the daring launching forth of conceptions in literature, inspired by them, soaring in highest regions." "Democratic Vistas," Holloway, *op. cit.*, p. 703-4.

[41] Yvor Winters, however, thinks that Whitman is guilty of the heresay of "imitative form." See *Primitivism and Decadence* (New York: Swallow Press & W. Morrow Co., 1947).

[42] Holloway, *op. cit.*, II, 90.

[43] "The Return of the Heroes," in "Autumn Rivulets."

[44] Jean Catel holds the view that Whitman's journalistic writings, before he began the *Leaves*, reveal a maladjusted young man, unsuccessful in the economic world, unsure of himself, unable to make social adjustments. Consequently, Whitman began to create a compensating world of fantasy and imagination, which found expression through his poems. Being in his conscious mind agitated by a sense of failure and frustration, he took refuge in poetic imagination. Jean Catel, *Walt Whitman: La Naissance du Poète* (Paris: Les Editions Reider, 1929). See Allen, *Whitman Handbook*, pp. 61-62.

a transformed attitude of mind. Whitman never set high value on a successful career or worldly aggrandizement; instead his aspiration had always been for the immortal. Looking back on his past life, he wrote in 1871:

> Walt Whitman is now 52 years old. No worldly aim has engrossed his life. He is still unmarried. None of the usual ardors of business ambition, of the acquisition of money, or the claims of society, pleasure, nor even the attractions of culture or art seemed to have enslaved him. The thought and the making of this work has spanned the whole horizon of his life, *almost since boyhood.*[45]

Furthermore, Whitman's realization of the transcendental self enabled him to overcome his inhibitions and helped the enlargement of his vision; the inversions of his sexual nature were transmuted into a spiritual passion for the mass of humanity. The view that Whitman was a split personality[46] cannot be accepted. There is no discoverable cleavage in him between his inner aspirations and outer environment. For him to whom value and existence became one there is little motive for inhibition. Similarly, Catel's interpretation that "the myself that Whitman 'celebrates' on each page . . . is the projection of the unconscious"[47] is a mistake. Whitman's "Me myself" is not the Freudian subconscious—which is a hideous debris of incestuous wishes and buried memories—but it is the self transmuted and exalted to the superliminal level. The subconscious is not the equivalent of the transcendental self.[48]

Whitman's life was a continued effort for self-elevation. If Whitman gained the supreme knowledge and achieved self-integration, it was by nothing short of an iron effort of will and a strenuous contemplation. Spiritual culture must be understood as an intense and sustained self-reflection, ceaseless watchfulness, and self-criticism. Only through meditative discipline (Dhyana Yoga) are the infinite rewards opened to us. Hence, it is only natural that Whitman puts so much emphasis on sanity, self-possession, and self-mastery. In "Democratic Vistas" he speaks of the cultivation of "a great masterful spirit"; echoing the

[45] *Complete Writings*, Vol. VI, Part I, No. 38.
[46] Hugh Fausset, *Walt Whitman: Poet of Democracy* (New Haven: Yale University Press, 1942). See *Whitman Handbook*, p. 83.
[47] Quoted in *Whitman Handbook*, p. 62.
[48] See Underhill, *Mysticism* (London: Methuen & Co., Ltd., 1919), p. 52.

Bhagvad Gita, he writes: "*A strong mastership of the general inferior self by the superior self*, is to be aided . . . by the literatus." [49]

The Hindu method of meditation (Dhyana Yoga), always held a certain fascination for Americans, particularly the transcendentalists. Thoreau practised yoga and speaks of it in *Walden* in explicit terms. He even styled himself a "Yogi." [50] In *Walden* he writes: "I know of no more encouraging fact than the unquestionable ability of man to elevate his life by a conscious endeavor." [51] Yoga, as the Vedantist understands it, is not an esoteric practice but meditative discipline, a focusing of consciousness. It is, in the words of the Gita, a conscious endeavor to "lift the self by the self." Only by such mental discipline can one develop the intuitive faculty, which alone will ultimately take one to the deep-lying essence beneath. Thoreau writes, "By a conscious effort of mind we can stand aloof from actions and their consequences; and all things, good and bad, go by us like a torrent. We are not wholly involved in nature." [52] Whitman, too, we have seen, possesses, in a supreme degree, this wonderful capacity for self-dissociation, for detaching himself from all surrounding activities, and what is more, for abstracting from the thoughts and experiences of his own mind. Whitman is conscious of a certain trance-like state leading to the suspension of the conscious intellect and accompanied by a strange feeling of exaltation and joy and a transformation, as it were, of the whole being; a state in which the mystic experiences a new awakening, the awakening of the spiritual vision, and, like the sage in the Upanishad, understands the being whose essence is joy. [53]

> In that condition the whole body is elevated to a state by others unknown —inwardly and outwardly illuminated, purified, made solid, strong, yet buoyant. A singular charm, more than beauty, flickers out of, and over, the face—a curious transparency beams in the eyes, . . .—the temper partakes also. Nothing that happens—no event, rencontre, weather, etc. —but it is confronted—nothing but is subdued into sustenance—such is the marvellous transformation from the old timorousness and the old process of causes and effects. *Sorrows and disappointments cease—there is*

[49] Holloway, *op. cit.*, p. 717. (Italics mine.) Cf. Gita, 6.6.
[50] Quoted in Arthur Christy, *The Orient in American Transcendentalism* (New York: Columbia University Press, 1932), p. 201.
[51] *Walden*, chap. ii.
[52] *Ibid.*, chap. v.
[53] See Taittiriya, 2.5.

*no more borrowing trouble in advance. A man realizes the venerable myth—
he is a god walking the earth*, he sees new eligibilities, powers and beauties
everywhere; *he himself has a new eyesight and hearing.* The play of the
body in motion takes a previously unknown grace. *Merely to move is then
a happiness, a pleasure—to breathe, to see, is also.* . . . All the beforehand
gratifications, drink, spirits, coffee grease, stimulants, mixtures, late
hours, luxuries, deeds of the night, seem as vexatious dreams, and
now the awakening;—many fall into their natural places, wholesome,
conveying diviner joys.[54]

Whitman, however, sometimes insists that during this state of meditation the "senses are not lost or counteracted" but maintained intact:

a trance, *yet with all the senses alert*—only a state of high exalted amusing
—*the tangible and material with all its shows, the objective world suspended
or surmounted for a while*, and powers in exaltation, freedom, vision—
*yet the senses not lost or counteracted.*[55]

But this should not be interpreted to mean that Whitman's mysticism
is "of a ranker, perhaps healthier stamp than that of Wordsworth, who
asserts: 'in that serene and blessed mood . . . we are laid asleep in body,
and become a living soul.'"[56] The "senses," which Whitman says are
not lost but maintained, are not the ordinary physical senses but the
"new eyesight and hearing" of which he speaks. They are the spiritual
sense or the inner vision which enables him to "retire" within the
inward abysms, with the "standards of the light and sense shut off"
and the objective world left behind.[57]

A comparison with the Hindu method of Yoga should bring to light
certain new facts about the meditative experiences through which
Whitman acquired final knowledge of the self. It may also offer us a
clue to Whitman's poetic method. Mercer has made an interesting
study of Walt Whitman and Raja Yoga, in which she points out
certain similarities between Whitman's meditative method and the
Yogic practices.[58] There is some evidence that Whitman underwent
certain of the experiences that usually accompany the practice of Yoga

[54] *Complete Writings*, IV, 26–27.
[55] Clifton Joseph Furness, *Walt Whitman's Workshop* (Cambridge: Harvard
University Press, 1928), p. 21.
[56] *Ibid.*, p. 21.
[57] *Ibid.*, n. 14.
[58] "Whitman on Raja Yoga," *Vedanta and the West*, XI (January-February,
1948), 26–31.

—if the term Yoga is understood in the sense indicated above. Distinction should, however, be made between Yoga as it is generally used, i.e., Dhyana Yoga, or the practice of meditation, and the Raja Yoga of Patanjali. Raja Yoga, with its dualistic assumptions, aims at extinguishing the state of consciousness, a complete extinction of all mental activity, whereas the Yogic method of Vedanta aims, through spiritual elevation, to transform the very stuff of our nature. Both methods involve, of course, in a greater or lesser degree, volitional effort and concentration of energy. But while in the former emphasis is laid exclusively on volition, the latter attaches greater importance to right knowledge and the cultivation of philosophic insight. The one depends on the strength of will, the other on the strength that comes of knowledge. In Raja Yoga we will away the alien elements to get at the soul; in the Yoga of Vedanta we realize the self by rejecting, through an intense self-reflection, the particular and finite with which it is wrongly identified. While Raja Yoga accords to nature a status independent of and separate from the *purusha* (person), Vedanta denies its separate existence and attempts to realize it as the non-dual *brahman*. The goal of Raja Yoga is *kaivalya*, or isolation, that of Vedanta identity (*sarvātmatva*) or universality.

The self of Whitman which says "it is not me myself" and which is conscious of its distinction from its surroundings, from the body, senses, and the like, which is untouched by sorrow and evil, and which stands apart and looks on—is not the *purusha* of *samkhya* (discrimination) and Raja Yoga—glorying in its isolation. It is not even like the self described in the Gita, 6, wherein the vision of the self is gained through the rather negative process of abstracting the attention from all outward manifestations of nature and suppressing the operations of the mind. Whitman's self is the dynamic, cosmic "I" of the Upanishads, the *atman-brahman*—attained through a process of universalizing the "ego," by meditating on the universal nature of the self, its at-oneness with the all. The highest experience, *brahmānubhava*, the Upanishads take not as the annihilation of the "I"—which is necessarily the case in Raja Yoga—but of its particularity and finitude. In fact, we realize the plenitude of our being as *bhūma*, whole. Through meditation on the whole, as "I am all, I am the Infinite Brahman," all particular consciousness is dissolved and the individual loses his particularity and becomes universal. The Chhandogya ordains: "That

I am all, so he must meditate."[59] This is the method of meditation, in identification, as distinguished from the Raja Yoga method of meditation, in isolation. Whitman evidently practised identification rather than isolation. We have in one of his notebooks a passage indicating the method of his meditation—a type of the "self-teaching exercises" that Whitman seems to have undergone deliberately.

> Abstract yourself from this book; realize where you are at present located, the point you stand that is now to you the centre of all. Look up overhead, *think of space stretching out, think of all the unnumbered orbs wheeling safely there,* invisible to us by day, some visible by night. . . . Spend some minutes faithfully in this exercise. Then again realize yourself upon the earth, at the particular point you now occupy. . . . (*thinks of four directions*). Seize these firmly in your mind, *pass freely over immense distances.* Turn your face a moment thither. Fix definitely the direction and the idea of the distances of separate sections of your own country, also of England, the Mediterranean sea, Cape Horn, the North Pole, and such like distant places.[60]

The Upanishads enjoin on us: "One should meditate upon the mind as Brahman; one should meditate upon Ākaśa (space) as Brahman,"[61] because the object of meditation is expansion and identification, and since both the mind and space are all-pervading and free from limitations, meditation on them will produce the expansion of the inner horizon.

It must not, however, be understood that the knowledge of the real nature of self can be gained without discriminating the self from the empirical objects and states with which it is wrongly perceived as associated, without stripping off the phenomenal attributes. Indra in Chhandogya, through a process of progressive elimination—not this, not this, which really means that the self is not any one particular object but is the undivided whole—reaches the conclusion that the self is not the body, not the breath, not the mind, but that it is beyond all thought, beginningless, birthless. This is not the same as the Raja Yoga method, because in the latter the opposition of the not-self is recognized as real, whereas in the method of Vedanta the not-self is rejected and negated. In Raja Yoga meditation takes the form of "I am not the

---

[59] Chhandogya, 2.21.4.
[60] *Complete Writings*, Vol. VI, Part II, No. 10.
[61] Chhandogya, 3.18.1.

not-self";[62] in Vedanta it ultimately assumes the form: "The not-self is my own self, I am all this." This, again, should not be mistaken for false identification—for false identification is identification with particular objects. (E.g., I am this object, I am that, which necessarily implies that I am not the other objects.) Its removal consists in establishing the consciousness that the self is all.

In the very act of meditating on its universal nature, the self gains the notion that it is the transcendental witness, the subject that can never become an object, that cannot be tainted by evil or suffering. Both acts are simultaneous. Intuitive identification and mystical abstraction are simultaneous processes, running parallel to each other. Even as the self knows itself as the transcendental subject, it expands and becomes all, because all particular reference has been eradicated and the barriers that separated the self from the not-self have been broken down. Similarly, in Whitman, too, both the processes run simultaneously. Whitman is aware of the distinction between his "Real Me" and the "not-Me" consisting of the natural surroundings and his surface consciousness. At the same time he feels his identity with all objects and processes of the world; he loafes and invites his soul, and lies at ease observing a spear of summer grass. This may be, as Mercer thinks, a phase of meditative discipline. Meditation it is, to be sure, but certainly not of the Raja Yogin's type.[63] This is meditation in identification, the practice of intuitive communion with the object wherein subject-object distinction is completely annulled. In Raja Yoga, too, at the stage of *samadhi* (absorption), subject-object notions drop away, and the mind becomes one with the object of its contemplation. But this type of identification is to be distinguished from intuitive identification. The practice of meditation in Raja Yoga is only an exercise for the mind, with the ultimate object of the complete dissolution of the mind, whereas in intuitive meditation identification is practised for the purpose of expanding the self, in order that the self may gain the consciousness of its identity with the world-all. In the Vedanta method again, the mind's vision is not limited to particular

[62] By a similar procedure, too, does the *pour-soi* (consciousness) of the existentialist constitute itself by separation from what is, the *en-soi*; but it is never felt as a certitude as its being is constantly in question, and is but a certain manner of not-being.

[63] Mercer evidently means by Raja Yoga the Yoga of the Gita, not the Yoga of Patanjali.

objects, but embraces in its expansive vision the totality of the universe; it spans the infinite, so to say. Moreover, the aim of Raja Yoga is not to achieve subject-object identity, but to restore and perfect their distinction which alone is real and primordially given. Accordingly, misery results from the false identification of the seer and the seen, and salvation consists in restoring the self to its primal oneness or isolation.

Whitman's egoism it was, to be sure, that furnished the motive for his mystical realizations. In the Upanishads the conception of the *atman* is built upon the ego-principle, or the I-sense (*ahamkāra*). According to them, the ego is not in conflict with the larger self or *atman*, but forms the basis for the attainment of selfhood. The method of the Upanishads is the method of *ahamgrahōpāsana* or magnification of the self. The Chhandogya speaks of the *ahamkārādesa* or the explanation by the ego. It asks us to meditate thus, "that I, indeed, am this whole world."[64] We are not asked to suppress the ego but to enlarge and sublimate it. What the Upanishads object to is our espousal of certain objects and aversion to certain others, which naturally results from the false notion of the limitation of our self. When we have realized the infinitude of our nature, our personality is said to have attained its highest fulfilment. The result of knowledge is identity with all; the result of ignorance is identity with finite things.[65]

[64] Chhandogya, 7.25.1.
[65] See Sankara's commentary on Brihadaranyaka, 4.3.20.

CHAPTER FIVE

# The Paradox of Identity

"And these tend inward to me, and I tend outward to them"
("Song of Myself," 15)

Most of Whitman's poems of the self, those of the earlier editions especially, may be read as dramatizations of the activity of the dynamic self. This activity of the self consists of a centrifugal and centripetal movement, a constant outgoing and return to the nucleus. While through the power of its intuitional sense the self negotiates with the cosmic manifold, quickly it withdraws into itself, like the snail into its shell. This self-merging and self-extricating activity is the way in which the dynamic self measures itself out and feels its own resilience. The symbolism of "merge" and "outlet" was perhaps suggested by the ideas of sexual union, with the female matrix as a nucleus from which issue forth the dual acts of mergence and outlet or birth. "This the nucleus—after the child is born of woman, man is born of woman, / This the bath of birth, this the merge of small and large, and the outlet again."[1] But it also suggests to the self its own nature of merger and extrication:

> This is the touch of my lips to yours, this the murmur of yearning,
> This the far-off depth and height reflecting my own face,
> This the thoughtful merge of myself, and the outlet again.[2]

That this resilience of the self is the characteristic mode of its being is made further explicit by the following lines:

> In me the caresser of life wherever moving, backward as well as
>     forward sluing,
> To niches aside and junior bending, not a person or object missing,
> Absorbing all to myself and for this song.[3]

[1] "I Sing the Body Electric," in "Children of Adam."
[2] "Song of Myself," 19.
[3] *Ibid.*, 13.

It is this mergence and outlet, the forward and backward movement of the soul that constitutes the dynamics of Whitman's poems. The drama of cosmic identification is followed by that of self-extrication. The poet who "wanders all night in my vision," dreaming "all dreams of the other dreamers," who traverses the whole span of the universe "speeding through space," through the heaven and the stars, and speeding with "tail'd meteors," who becomes by turns the bride, the bridegroom, the hounded slave, and "the sleepless widow looking out on the winter midnight" quickly abstracts himself from the real or imagined spectacle and from his own experience. Though participating in world action, he remains unattached. He is "in and out of the game" and knows that the objects are not the "Me myself"; he stands "apart from the pulling and hauling." He looks on his own "crucifixion and bloody crowning." In the passage on the hounded slave in the "Song of Myself," 33, after living the experience of the hounded slave the poet casts it off like a garment only to put it on again: "Agonies are one of my changes of garments." Again, he projects himself into an "asker" and sits shamefaced and begs, but soon rises ecstatic through all. Like some elusive substance,

> Another self, a duplicate of every one, skulking and hiding it goes,
> Formless and wordless through the streets of the cities, polite and
>     bland in the parlors,
> In the cars of the railroads, in steamboats, in the public assembly,
> .   .   .   .   .   .   .   .   .   .   .   .
> Keeping fair with the customs, speaking not a syllable of itself.
> Speaking of any thing else but never of itself.[4]

The self which merges itself in all existence and says, "All these I feel or am," with equal facility departs from "materials": "I am as one disembodied, triumphant, dead."[5] While the self feels its power through identification with cosmic existence, it asserts its transcendental nature and its sovereignty by extrication. "Myself moving forward then and now and forever / . . . Infinite and omnigenous."[6] In its state of interiority and "centripetency" the soul stands imperturbable, "pois'd on itself," "aplomb in the midst of irrational things." "I Hear America Singing" (Inscriptions) derives its force from the First Person Singular (as most other poems do), and establishes the

[4] "Song of the Open Road," 13.
[5] "So Long," in "Songs of Parting."
[6] "Song of Myself," 32.

"I" at the center of the vision. The "Children of Adam" poems project the self as the Adamic archetype:

> Ages and ages returning at intervals,
> Undestroy'd, wandering immortal,
> Lusty, phallic . . .
> I, chanter of Adamic songs,
> Through the new garden the West, the great cities,
> Deliriate. . . .

Or again in "To the Garden the World":

> Existing I peer and penetrate still,
> Content with the present, content with the past,
> By my side or back of me Eve following . . .

The poem "Me Imperturbe" (Inscriptions) sketches with extreme vividness the "posture" of the transcendental self "standing at ease in Nature" with perfect aplomb. Whitman's self-celebration is often presented in terms of a "dramatic gesture"; it is dramatically envisioned and rendered.

> here the
> flame of materials,
> Here spirituality the translatress. . . .
> . . . . . . .
> Yes here comes my mistress the soul.

"Flame of materials" is a keen visualization; the sensation is intensely felt and registered. Some of the poems are a dialogue with the soul, and often employ the dramatic voice as a technical device.

> Come, said my soul,
> Such verses for my body let us write, (for we are one,)
> That should I after death invisibly return,
> Or, long, long hence, in other spheres,
> There to some group of mates the chants resuming,
> . . . . . . .
> Signing for soul and body, set to them my name,
>                                     WALT WHITMAN

This constant oscillation between the "I" and the observed world, outward expansion and withdrawal to the center is a feature of nearly all of Whitman's successful poems,[7] and accounts for the dramatic

---

[7] See David Daiches in Milton Hindus, *Leaves of Grass One Hundred Years After* (Stanford, Calif.: Stanford University Press, 1955).

quality of many of their lines. While some poems, like "Salut au Monde," "Starting from Paumanok," and "The Sleepers" are purely poems of expansion, others, like "To You," are poems purely of self-extrication. The self is parted aside from the "mockeries," and "stands forth out of affairs, out of commerce, shops, works, forms," and the like, its own "master or mistress." In yet other lines the sense of mystical abstraction and absorption in the object are simultaneously present in a given moment of experience. "I loafe and invite my soul. / I lean and loafe at my ease observing a spear of summer grass."[8] This is a species of intuitive communion with the object wherein the poet contemplates a spear of summer grass in an illumined state of self-awareness. Similarly, in the following lines the poet is absorbed in an experience at the same time that he is withdrawn from it: "The scene and all its belongings, how they seize and affect me, / ... Myself effusing and fluid, a phantom curiously floating, now here absorb'd and arrested."[9]

Also characteristic of this to and fro motion is the alternation between kinetic and "depth" images, between "efflux" and "influx," flow and fixity. While the kinetic symbols like space, time, and sea set the self in motion upon its centrifugal journeys, the "depth" symbols mark its return to the center. "A Song of Joys" opens with the spirit's outward expansion, which, quite characteristically, the poet describes in terms of astronomical imagery:

> O the joy of my spirit—it is uncaged—it darts like lightning!
> It is not enough to have this globe or a certain time,
> I will have thousands of globes and all time.

Here space and time are realized as symbols of the spirit's dynamism. The poet celebrates the joys of the universe. But this embracing movement is quickly followed by the return of the spirit to its own center. The soul is "vibrated" back from the objects to its own nucleus and sits "pois'd on itself."

> O the joy of my soul leaning pois'd on itself, receiving identity through materials and loving them, observing characters and absorbing them,

[8] "Song of Myself," I.
[9] "Sparkles from the Wheel," in "Autumn Rivulets."

> My soul vibrated back to me from them, from sight, hearing, touch,
> reason, articulation, comparison, memory and the like.

Realizing its pure "immaterial" nature, the soul withdraws itself into
its center and turns its vision inward: "My body done with materials,
my sight done with my material eyes." But quickly following is a
typical space symbol marking the spirit's re-emergence into the outer
expanse:

> O to realize space!
> The plenteousness of all, that there are no bounds,
> To emerge and be of the sky, of the sun and moon and flying clouds,
>     as one with them.

Again, the poet reverts to the idea of depth and interiority: "To these
proud laws of the air, the water and the ground, proving my interior
soul impregnable, / And nothing exterior shall ever take command of
me." Close upon this comes again the symbol of motion and fluidity:

> O to sail to sea in a ship!
> To leave this steady unendurable land,
> To leave the tiresome sameness of the streets, the sidewalks and the
>     houses,
> To leave you O you solid motionless land, and entering a ship,
> To sail and sail and sail!

It is through such an alternation of kinetic and depth symbols that the
poet dramatizes the central paradox of the dynamic self, which while
being its own center or core, expands into the cosmic whole, thus
realizing its extreme elasticity.

The opening of Section 33 of "Song of Myself" shows how contemplation of kinetic images releases the dynamic self and sends it
upon its centrifugal voyages. All "ties and ballasts" being loosened,
the giant self travels and sails.

> Space and Time! now I see it is true, what I guess'd at,
> What I guess'd when I loaf'd on the grass,
>
> · · · · · · · · · · ·
>
> My ties and ballasts leave, my elbows rest in sea-gaps,
> I skirt sierras, my palms cover continents,
> I am afoot with my vision.

The soul vies with the speeding astronomical bodies, "expanding always expanding, outward and outward and forever outward." But it soon rises superior to them and outruns them. "My sun has his sun and round him obediently wheels."[10] Similarly, after identifying himself with the speeding stallion, the poet says,

> I but use you a moment, then I resign you, stallion,
> Why do I need your paces when I myself outgallop them?
> Even as I stand or sit passing faster than you.[11]

Thus, in images suggesting motion, traveling, sailing, speeding, and the like, the poet finds symbolic actions expressive of the soul's dynamism. The image of the sailing ship, which is a recurrent one in *Leaves of Grass*, has a peculiar hold on his mind, as it suggests to him the vision of his own voyaging soul, as in "The Ship Starting":

> Lo, the unbounded sea,
> On its breast a ship starting, spreading all sails, carrying even her moonsails,
> The pennant is flying aloft as she speeds she speeds so stately—below emulous waves press forward,
> They surround the ship with shining curving motions and foam.[12]

The images of "A Song of the Rolling Earth" similarly suggests to the poet the motion, the stateliness and poise of his own soul: "The divine ship sails the divine sea."[13] The open road is also seen as a dynamic symbol that liberates the soul from all restraints and aids its expansive activity. "From his hour I ordain myself loos'd of limits and imaginary lines."[14] Hence, the open road expresses the dynamic soul "better than I express myself."

[10] "Song of Myself," 45.

[11] "Song of Myself," 32.

[12] "The Ship Starting," in "Inscriptions"; also "Sail Out for Good, Eidólon Yacht!" in "Good-Bye My Fancy." Also, from "By the Roadside,"

> Gliding o'er all, through all,
> Through Nature, Time, and Space,
> As a ship on the waters advancing,
> The voyage of the soul—not life alone,
> Death, many deaths I'll sing.

And from "Aboard at a Ship's Helm," in "Sea-Drift,"

> But O the ship, the immortal ship! O ship aboard the ship!
> Ship of the body, ship of the soul, voyaging, voyaging, voyaging.

[13] "A Song of the Rolling Earth," last line of section 1.

[14] "Song of the Open Road." See Allen's interesting study of Whitman's "long journey" motif in *The Journal of English and Germanic Philology*, XXXVIII

"Passage to India" is one of the finest of Whitman's poems in which the dynamic symbols are most fully exploited. The poem is also interesting in that it marks out clear transitions through which a physical event, namely the opening of the passage to India, is first transformed into an image presenting an emotional complex and then given a deliberate symbolic purpose. Thus, the structure of the poem[15] consists of the dramatic progression of a theme through three well-marked phases. The poem opens with a celebration of modern wonders, the Suez Canal, the "mighty railroad" and the transatlantic cable. But in lines 8–9, which mark the first transition, these physical events assume a rich emotional significance and are transformed into the evocative image of passage or a bridge joining the present with the past, the New World with the Old. The emotion excited by the image is indeed so intense that the poet bursts forth into an ecstasy: "Yet first to sound, and ever sound, the cry with thee O soul. / The Past! the Past! the Past!" In Section 2 of the poem, passage to India emerges clearly as an image and is elaborated through Sections 2–7. The poet sees in the modern achievements the fulfilment of a divine purpose, and of man's "long probation."

> The oceans to be cross'd, the distant brought near,
> The lands to be welded together.
>
> .    .    .    .    .    .
>
> But in God's name, and for thy sake O soul.

Physical events take on a spiritual significance as they promise the accomplishment of a world mystically united into a "rondure." In Section 5 the image of passage to India fuses into the newly emerged image of the "vast rondure" of the world "swimming in space," which itself becomes a rich dynamic symbol in which the poet perceives an

---

(January, 1939), 76–95: reprinted in *Walt Whitman—as Man, Poet, and Legend*, pp. 62–83. The "long journey" theme, which was also a common Romantic metaphor, as Allen observes, may be best interpreted as a symbolic expression of the Dynamic Self.

[15] See James E. Miller's analysis of the poem in *A Critical Guide to "Leaves of Grass"* (Chicago: University of Chicago Press, 1957). Also critical note on the poem in Gay Wilson Allen and Charles T. Davis, *Walt Whitman's Poems* (New York: New York University Press, 1955). For other critical analyses see Stanley K. Coffman, Jr., "Form and Meaning in Whitman's 'Passage to India,'" *PMLA*, LXX (June, 1955), 337–47, and Clare R. Goldfarb, "The Poet's Role in 'Passage to India,'" *Walt Whitman Review*, VIII, No. 4 (December, 1962), 75–79.

analogy to his dynamic soul, "Now first it seems my thought begins to span thee." Through Sections 6 and 7 the substantive image of passage receives rich elaboration. Section 8 marks the second transition and the climax of the poem. This transition represents the transformation of the passage motif into the symbolic voyage of the dynamic self. Passage to India is transformed into passage to more than India (Section 9); the geographical "rondure" swimming in space is transcended by the image of the soul sailing through "Time and Space and Death, like waters flowing" (Section 8). This third phase of the passage motif has already been hinted at toward the end of Section 7 in the lines, "O soul, I with thee and thou with me, / Thy circumnavigation of the world begin" But it is in the opening lines of Section 8 that the image of passage emerges clearly as a symbol of the soul's dynamism.

> O we can wait no longer,
> We too take ship O soul,
> Joyous we too launch out on trackless seas.

In this image of the soul setting sail "athwart the shapeless vastness of space" (Section 8), the symbolic value of the passage motif is fully realized. The dynamic soul emerges as a supreme navigator.

> And lo, thou gently masterest the orbs,
> Thou matest Time, smilest content at Death,
> And fillest, swellest full the vastnesses of Space.

And in the ecstatic conclusion passage itself, which at the level of the image is but a means to an end, becomes the mode of existence of the exploring soul.

> O my brave soul!
> O farther farther sail!
> O daring joy, but safe! are they not all the seas of God!
> O farther, farther, farther sail!

Whitman's constant enactment of "merger" and "extrication" is a way of presenting the mystical intuition of the unitary self. The centrifugal-centripetal oscillation between the "I" and the world emphasizes this intuitive identity of being, and at the same time establishes the self as the center, the static reference or "still point" of this dynamics. For all its dynamism the self never loses sight of itself as an observer and experiencer, as a transcendental subject. It has been argued that Whitman is obsessed with the concepts of endless progression and succession, and that his poems give us the feeling rather of "disintegration" than of unity.[16] There is no doubt a preponderance of kinetic images in the poems, but these are effectively offset by notions of centrality and depth. Strange as it may seem, the perpetual symbolic voyages and endless processions constantly refer back to the "still point" at the center. This central paradox of fixity in motion and oneness in the many is implicit in Whitman's conception of the self. Whitman sees the whole universe as but an emanation of the creative self: "The universe is in myself—it shall pass through me as a procession."[17] And again, "Through me the afflatus surging and surging, through me the current and index."[18] It is of this principle of stability in motion, of changelessness amidst change that Emerson is speaking in these lines:

> Yet this incessant movement and progression which all things partake could never become sensible to us but by contrast to some principle of fixture or stability in the soul. While the eternal generation of circles proceeds, the eternal generator abides. That central life is somewhat superior to creation, superior to knowledge and thought and contains all its circles.[19]

The Gita affirms the transcendent nature of the self, the experiencing subject who is beyond event: "I am not in them, they are in me."[20]

This concept of the self enclosing all is not one of unity-in-diversity, but a one-and-many paradox in which the onefold and the manifold are beheld simultaneously, the manifold being but an aspect, a reflection of the one. This idea is brought out in the Upanishadic analogy: "The Self is beheld onefold and manifold simultaneously like the moon reflected in water."[21] The concept of unity-in-diversity is held as a valid concept only when diversity is made the condition of unity, or in other words, when it is dialectically justified. Whitman's dynamism

---

[16] See Harry B. Read, "The Heraclitan Obsession of Whitman," *Personalist*, Vol. XV (April, 1934).

[17] *Complete Writings of Walt Whitman* (New York: G. P. Putnam's Sons, 1902), Vol. VI, Part I, No. 49.

[18] "Song of Myself," 24.

[19] "Circles."

[20] Gita, 7.12.

[21] Amrita Bindu Upanishad, 11–12.

is not a compulsive activity arising from an inner necessity, as it is in the dialectical becoming but is a free self-indulgence (*leela* or play) flowing out of the plenitude of being. The incessant motion that his poems enact is a purely symbolic act, freed from the congealing effects of time and space—the ordinary psychological categories—an act that becomes a mode of existence. Paradoxically, this motion produces no change and causes nothing to happen; and it is not a movement toward a desired destination but is motion as a mode of dynamic being. It is a mode in which the poet's intuition, "the fluid and swallowing soul," operates by dissolving the subject-object barriers, as in "Song of Myself," 20, "To me the converging objects of the universe perpetually flow." Or as he says in "The Sleepers," "The diverse shall be no less diverse, but they shall flow and unite—they unite now." Whitman's "fluid" images convey the notion of a vast spiritual continuum, the "eternal float" of which "Crossing Brooklyn Ferry" is a most beautiful symbolization. The concepts of time and space, no doubt, exert a fascination upon the poet's mind. But these concepts are apprehended not as the oppressive categories of discrete time and place, the time of tenses and the space of distances, but as symbols of dynamism in which all divisions are merged into the living essence of the present. Thus, Whitman's universe, though constantly marching, is a changeless order, an eternity of sameness.

Charles Feidelson's view[22] that Whitman is concerned with process or exploration as a mode of existence and that his poetry records a shift from the categories of "substance" to those of "process" is an adequate description of Whitman's dynamism. But while Feidelson rightly emphasizes the symbolic nature of Whitman's voyages, he fails to appreciate the presence in all his poems of a static point of view, namely, the self, which is itself not a process, but the protagonist of a ceaseless action. It can be seen that Whitman presents "dynamism" under two aspects, as a mode of being, and as an evolutionary process by which visible objects constantly ripen into spiritual results. Poems like "Song of Myself" and "The Sleepers" dramatize dynamism under the first aspect, as a mode of existence of the soul, which remains changeless and self-identical, performing roles and enacting the drama of identification. But, as I have suggested above, Whitman also views

[22] Charles Feidelson, *Symbolism and American Literature* (Chicago: University of Chicago Press, 1953), pp. 16–27.

dynamism as a world process. This dual aspect is clearly brought out in the poem "Eidólons" (in "Inscriptions"). Of dynamism as pertaining to the material world, Whitman says:

> Ever the mutable,
> Ever materials, changing, crumbling, re-cohering,
> Ever the ateliers, the factories divine,
> Issuing eidólons.

The material process consists of an endless mutation, or a cyclic or "orbic" tendency shaping eidólons or spiritual images. But "process" itself as a dynamic concept is attractive to the expansive soul, so the poet says: "And thee my soul, / Joys, ceaseless exercises, exaltations." As an eidólon or the spiritual principle, the soul is the "purport and end" of all visible material process. It has the paradoxical nature of remaining changeless amidst flux.

> Unfix'd yet fix'd,
> Ever shall be, ever have been and are,
> Sweeping the present to the infinite future,
> Eidólons, eidólons, eidólons.

The following lines from the "Song of Myself," 32, further confirm the idea of the self subsisting beyond time and change:

> I wonder where they got these tokens,
> Did I pass that way huge times ago and negligently drop them?
> Myself moving forward then and now and forever.

Again, the poet believes that his self will pass through cycles of transmigratory existence: "Believing I shall come again upon the earth after five thousand years." [23]

It should, then, be appreciated that underlying all Whitman's poems is a stabilizing principle, namely, the self, which being the protagonist of all action is the principle of unity and organization in the poems. This is not, however, to claim that the poet always builds up a strict dramatic unity as in the "Lilacs." The catalogues of the longer poems are generally miscellaneous and lacking in organization, the choice of their detail is arbitrary, and the transitions between sections and within each section are abrupt. Nevertheless, the self of these poems constitutes what little unity of theme and tone they may

[23] "Song of Myself," 43.

possess and imposes on them an over-all dramatic frame. Thus, these poems may be roughly described as dramatizations in as much as they celebrate the heroics of the soul and are essentially all "songs of myself." Besides, the constant drama of "merge" and "extrication" they enact lends them the tone of dramatic performance, though they may lack a narrative structure and do not record a temporal progression of events. The structure of "Song of Myself" may be examined in the light of these observations. Feidelson is of the opinion that the poem lacks a stabilizing factor. "Whatever the nominal subject, it is soon lost in sheer 'process'; all roads lead into the 'Song of Myself,' in which the bare Ego interacts with a miscellaneous world. The result is Whitman's characteristic disorder and turgidity."[24] While it must frankly be admitted that the poem is loosely organized and lacks a strict dramatic structure, it is not difficult to discover in it an underlying principle of organization. The entire poem is a "performance" of the dynamic self; and it may be seen to be of the structure of a paradox—the paradox of identity.[25] The dual tendencies of self-merger and self-extrication by which the self is dramatized form this structure, and the cosmic inventories of which the self is the "omnific" animating principle serve the double purpose of "demarcating" and "identifying" the self. This structure may be represented diagrammatically:

PARADOX OF IDENTITY
Centrifugal
"Always a knit of identity": "All these I feel or am"

"I"
The felt unity $\longleftarrow$ $\longrightarrow$ Object

"Always distinction"; "They are not the Me myself"
Centripetal

Notable among those critics who have attempted to examine the structure of "Song of Myself," are Carl F. Strauch, James E. Miller, Malcolm Cowley, and Gay Wilson Allen.[26] We may examine their

[24] *Op. cit.*
[25] I have borrowed this phrase from Richard Chase, *Walt Whitman Reconsidered* (New York: William Sloane, 1955), though here I put it to my own use.
[26] Carl F. Strauch, "The Structure of Walt Whitman's 'Song of Myself,'" *English Journal* (College edition), XXVII (September, 1938), 597–607; Miller, *op. cit.*; Cowley, Introduction to *Leaves of Grass*, The First Edition (New York: Viking Press, 1959); Gay Wilson Allen, *Walt Whitman Handbook* (New York: Hendricks House, Inc., 1957), p. 117; Allen and Davis, *op. cit.*, Introduction, pp. 5–9.

opinions briefly in this context. Strauch's sketch of a logical development in the poem depends on an arbitrary division of the poem into
five paragraphs or logical steps. These divisions do not convincingly
trace any logical advancement of thought, and they overlap. For example, we wonder whether the third paragraph (Sections 26–38),
entitled "Life flowing in upon the self, then evolutionary interpenetration of life," marks any distinctive advance upon the first paragraph,
"Mystical interpenetration of the self with all life and experience, and
whether the two phases are really different at all. Similarly, Miller
attempts with no better success to discover in what seems to be a
static frame a step-by-step progression in the "Mystic Way." Since
the different mystical phases do not follow strictly in the order
described by Evelyn Underhill in *Mysticism*, Miller calls the poem
an "inverted mystical experience." While I am in complete agreement
with Miller's emphasis that the poem has an "informing idea" or a
"center of relevancy," and that it is a dramatic representation of a
mystical experience, my objection to his analysis is that the division
of the poem into seven mystical phases is, as in the former case,
arbitrary and forces the poem into a predetermined mould. To illustrate, there is no clear progression in the poem from "entry into the
mystical state" (the first phase) to emergence from it (the last phase).
The very first line of the poem, "I celebrate myself," may be interpreted as a state of emergence. The union or the final stage of the
mystical experience in which the poet has a supreme perception of
eternal being, which according to Miller occurs in Sections 44–49
may be said to occur in the following lines of Section 3: "There was
never any more inception than there is now, / . . . Nor any more
heaven or hell than there is now," and "I am satisfied—I see, dance,
laugh, sing." Or in these lines of Section 20:

> I exist as I am, that is enough,
> If no other in the world be aware I sit content,
> And if each and all be aware I sit content.

Or in such lines of Section 24 as "Divine am I inside and out" or "I
dote on myself," which give intimations of the exultation of being.
It may be questioned further whether there is any discernible difference
in tone, form, or content between Section 15, which in his analysis
comes under the second phase "awakening of self," and Section 33,

which comes under the fourth phase "illumination and dark night of the soul"; and also whether the poem records phases like the "purification of self" and the "dark night of the soul." Whitman's identification with the sinful and the suffering may not be the "dark night of the soul," as Miller thinks, but the self's detached participation in the world's experience. The fact of the case is that the climax of utterance occurs in the cryptic opening lines of the poem; and the central meaning of the whole poem is implicit in these lines, and through successive accumulations it merely expands in bulk as it were, without recording any advance in thought, or any growth except in the spatial sense. The poem proceeds by the ramification of a single central theme; and this is true of many other poems of Whitman like "A Song for Occupations," "Salut au Monde," etc. Again, the poem does not seem to be arranged in the narrative order of a "moment of ecstasy" followed by a "sequel," as has been suggested by Cowley. If it were so, the ecstasy, which according to Cowley occurs in the second sequence (Section 5) should have occurred as a condition precedent of the state in which the poet affirms, "I celebrate myself." For how can the poet celebrate a self that is yet to be discovered or awakened, and how can he further affirm its identity with the "you," the other, unless he has already realized its true nature, which is non-different from the not-self? In the fifth chant the poet is evidently speaking of his ecstasy in retrospect. Mr. Cowley's statement that the "Song of Myself" "comes closer to being a rhapsody or tone poem, one that modulates from theme to theme, often changing in key and tempo, but always preserving its unity of feeling as it moves onward in a wave-like flow" is perhaps a more accurate characterization of the structure of the poem. But his additional statement that it has a "firm narrative structure" with its parts following one another "in an irreversible order, like the beginning, middle and end of any good narrative," and his attempt to divide the poem into nine sequences does violence, as the previous analyses do, to the form of the poem by forcing upon it a pattern that is not there. The objections that we have raised against the former views may be taken here, too. To cite one such objection: the power of identification which, according to Cowley, forms the sixth sequence (Sections 30–38) is most dramatically expressed in the opening lines of the first chant itself and in the meditative communion with the "spear of summer grass" and can be shown to run through

Sections 15 and 16, or for that matter through almost any section of the poem. According to Cowley's analysis, Sections 1–4 of the poem serve as a sort of exordium or introduction to the narrative, and beginning with Section 5, the ecstasy, the theme is given a narrative development. There is no doubt that the opening in Section 1 and the close in the last two triplets of the last section are well marked by their distinct tones, but it is difficult to trace through the poem a strict narrative development. In the light of the foregoing analysis it would seem that the poem does not lend itself to any division based on thematic progression. Allen's suggestion that the poem has a spatial rather than a logical form that builds by successive accumulation of images in a spatial order is perhaps the most accurate statement of the problem. The poem has no doubt a dramatic situation but no development, a unity of feeling but no strict narrative order. It may be described as a prolonged enactment of a single static situation, namely, the paradox of identity. Cowley is perfectly right in asserting that the poem has a unity "in tone and image and direction." But, as I have pointed out, the climax of the situation comes at the very opening of the poem, there are, in fact, several such moments of climax, so that neither thought nor emotion really advances. The gross paradoxical form in which the poem is cast allows for no real logical growth nor dramatic development. However, the tension of the "coinciding opposites" constituting this structure generates motion, and thus renders the presentation dramatic. The paradox itself as a rhetorical device is a startlingly dramatic way of presenting an idea.

By way of illustrating the points made above, I may attempt a brief section-by-section analysis of the theme of the poem, "Song of Myself." [27]

Section 1: A cryptic affirmation of the identity of the transpersonal self and meditative communion.

Section 2: The feeling of health and fullness and ecstasy of being. The self exudes health. The "song of me" rising—an effusion of the soul. The self the origin of all poems.

Section 3: Eternal now and the paradox of the dynamic urge. The paradox of identity and distinction. The not-self negated. The mystery of being: "I and this mystery." The joy and fullness of mystical being.

[27] Here I follow the text of the 1855 edition.

Section 4: The transcendental self extricated: "But they are not the Me myself." The detached participant and witness.

Section 5: Ecstasy and union.

Section 6: The ever recurring grass—a symbol of democratic equality and the immortality of the soul.

Section 7: Self, the immortal essence and self of all: "all just as immortal."

Section 8: Self: the transcendental witness: "I mind them or the resonance of them. . . . I come again and again."

Section 9: Identification.

Section 10: Self: absorption in being: "wandering amazed at my own lightness and glee," and witness consciousness.

Section 11: Self: the witness and the invisible presence: "An unseen hand also passed over their bodies."

Section 12: Self: the witness.

Section 13: Self: the witness consciousness and the "caresser of life."

Section 14: Self: the witness.

Section 15: The transcendental witness and the drama of identification.

Section 16: Drama of identification. The self is "of every hue and trade and rank, of every caste and religion."

Section 17: Wisdom: the emanation of the soul. Self: the transpersonal essence.

Section 18: The all-embracing wisdom annuls the sense of opposition.

Section 19: The all-embracing self.

Section 20: The universal nature of the self affirmed. The self transcendent and self-existent. It is its own world: "One world is aware, and by far the largest to me, and that is myself."

Section 21: The inclusive nature of the self affirmed. "A chant of dilation or pride." Merger.

Section 22: The inclusive self—the paradox of identity—annuls pairs of opposites.

Section 23: The self extricated from "the facts." "They are not my dwelling. . . . I enter by them to an area of the dwelling."

Section 24: Self-merger: "Through me many long dumb voices." And self-exultation: "I dote on myself."

Section 25: Merger and extrication: "My final merit I refuse you." The self affirmed: "plenum of proof."

Section 26: The transcendental subject. Identification and ecstasy of being.

Section 27: Merger and ecstasy.

Section 28, 29: Senses and self-conquest.

Section 30: The sense of being.

Section 31: The drama of identification.

Section 32: Identification and extrication. The self affirmed.

Section 33: The giant self or *virāt rūpa* (cosmic form) and the drama of cosmic identification.

Section 34, 35, 36: Self the detached spectator.

Section 37: Identification and extrication: "These become mine and me every one," yet the self rises "extatic through all."

Section 38: Extrication and abstraction from experience. The prowess of the self. The vision that stretches beyond time and space. The ubiquitous presence of the self.

Section 39: Self: the Answerer.

Section 40, 41: The prowess of the Self: the Superman and creator.

Section 42: Identification and extrication.

Section 43: The self rising through cycles of existence. Extrication.

Section 44: The self through cycles of evolution.

Section 45: Self: cosmic dynamism.

Section 46: Self: dynamism: "I tramp a perpetual journey."

Section 47: The teacher.

Section 48: The self affirmed.

Section 49: The self persisting through cycles of deaths and births.

Section 50: The ecstasy of being.

Section 51: Self: the volatile essence that comes and goes.

Section 52: Cosmic expansion and departure.

From the above description it may be seen that the poem does not lend itself to any division into sequences or phases of dramatic development. The various segments of the poem overlap, and there is constant repetition of themes, which makes a dramatic progression impossible. It should further become clear that these segments are not arranged in an irreversible order to make a temporal structure possible, but are fitted together rather in a straggling fashion. Roger Asselineau's suggestion[28] that the poem has the resemblance of a mosaic is perhaps

[28] Quoted in Allen and Davis, *op. cit.*, p. 8. Cf. also Roy Harvey Pearce's analysis of the structure of the poem in *The Continuity of American Poetry* (Prince-

a correct description of its structure. Notwithstanding this loose arrangement, the poem possesses a unity in theme, tone, and image. It is an epic of the self set in the framework of heroic and cosmic concepts, comparable in its expansive quality to *Paradise Lost*, or better yet, the heroic Song of Krishna in the Bhagavad-Gita.

## II

Whitman's democratic faith is born out of his conception of the mystical self. Since the central problem of democracy is the resolution of the inherent conflict between the individual and the universe, Whitman resolves it at the level of the transpersonal self, where the individual being himself is also the self of all. At the core of his being the individual is one with the cosmic whole. The inner and the outer coincide in the self. Your own self is the self of all. Herein is the paradox of individual identity, which is also the paradox of democracy. The purpose of democracy as a form of government is the cultivation of individualism, "the divine pride of man in himself." For it is only by forming great individuals that a harmonious society is possible. Without the realization of the inner identity of all selves no amount of ordering and discipline from outside can bring about a harmonious society. The faith that there is a central identity of self running through all life is the foundation of democracy and freedom. Each individual is unique, and yet he is identical with the all. It is this conviction of the uniqueness and intrinsic worth of every human being that accounts for Whitman's individualism and his espousal of democracy as the surest guarantee of individual values. In Whitman's opinion individualism is indispensable to democracy, as without it democracy is of no avail.

---

ton, 1961), pp. 69–83. Pearce, to my mind, states the problem correctly when he remarks that the poem evinces no structure with an "internal-external sense of necessity," "no scheme whereby we may decide that a given section should or should not have begun where it begins and ended where it ends, or contain what it contains." The poem has a "movement," but not a "form"—a "movement of sensibility" resembling the process of "hypnogogic meditation, controlled not by rules or method but by the intensely personal pulsations and periodicities of the meditative act." "Such pulsations and periodicities are expressions of the energy of the creative self. . . ." Pearce calls this variety an "adamic poem," as distinct from the "mythic poem" (of Eliot)—a type in which there is only an adamic naming of things "related only by the force of the poetic ego operative on them," and little or no dramatic effect. (*ibid.*, p. 166.)

Since individualism is the basic motif of Whitman's writings, a comparison with Hegel's opinion on this question will bring into sharp relief Whitman's conception of the individual. The Hegelian logic allows for the individual man but a subordinate position and ultimately leads to totalitarianism by sacrificing the individual interests to the higher purposes of the aggregate. In Hegel individuals exist as mutually related parts of the whole and as such have no independent status. As a part the individual is merely instrumental to the other parts. Treated in abstraction, he loses his significance, because what little significance he has he acquires only by virtue of the context of the whole in which he appears. Value resides in the whole rather than in the parts. The individual by himself is incomplete, partial, hence unreal. Accordingly, the citizen of a state exists as part of a valuable whole, and isolated he becomes worthless. He is valued not for his own sake but for the contribution he makes toward the excellence and reality of the whole. The doctrine of internal relations also points to the same conclusion. The individual selves being members of an organism cannot retain their uniqueness, as they are mutually determined and transformed by each other. Their very nature is formed by the externality, the rest of the universe. An individual's relation to other individuals goes to constitute his being, and the nature of the universe, which is the whole, forms an essential ingredient in his own nature. This logic leads Hegel to believe that ultimate reality and value rest in the state, "The state is the actually existing realized moral life." "For his [individual's] spiritual reality consists in this, that his own essence—Reason—is objectively present to him, that it possesses objective immediate existence for him. . . . For truth is the unity of the universal and subjective will, and the universal is to be found in the State, in its laws, its universal and rational arrangements. The State is the Divine Idea as it exists on earth." [29] The state is thus a miniature model of the absolute, and the members living in it are its partial representations, existing for the sake of the state, subserving its ends, and contributing toward its self-enrichment. Thus, in Hegel's scheme the individual man has an instrumental, not an intrinsic value. He is prized not for his own sake, but as a means to the community.

[29] Bertrand Russell, *A History of Western Philosophy* (New York: Simpson & Schuster, 1945).

This conception of Hegel's stands in sharp contrast to the Vedantic conception, according to which each individual is a complete entity by himself, self-sufficient and self-contained. The individual does not depend for his reality on his being related to something external to himself. Reality is not contained in external relationships, it is wrapped up in one's own being.[30] Man is not moulded and determined by external laws. He is a law unto himself.[31] Relationships cannot express his real nature, which is unique and "indivisible." Each individual possesses a uniqueness and impenetrability which can be affected by no amount of influx from outside. "To these proud laws of the air, the water and the ground, proving my interior soul impregnable, / And nothing exterior shall ever take command of me."[32] Each self is an "identity," as Whitman expresses it, "self-poised," "soaring its own flight, following out itself."[33] Whitman speaks of "the pride and completion of man in himself."[34] The individual is not instrumental to anything else; everything else is instrumental to him. He does not tend outward; all else tends to him. He is not complemented by the "other"; he stands in his self-completion and centripetal isolation.[35] As such, every human being is "divine in his own right."[36] He is "sole and untouchable by any canons of authority,"[37] laws of the community, or acts of state legislature. He derives his value not by virtue of any extraneous circumstance, but from his own intrinsic nature. "I am he who places over you no master, owner, better, God, beyond what waits intrinsically in yourself."[38] The individual man is valued and reverenced not for his "extrinsic acquirements or position,"[39] but for the "ever-reserved right of a deathless individuality,"[40] for that "something" in him, "the inherent soul," which being in

[30] "Lodged in the inmost recess," Katha, 2.12.

[31] *svarāt*, Chhandogya, 7.25.2.

[32] "A Song of Joys."

[33] Emory Holloway, *Complete Poetry and Selected Prose and Letters* (London: Nonesuch, 1938), p. 706.

[34] *Complete Writings*, Vol. VI, Part I, No. 26.

[35] "Individuality, the pride and centripetal isolation of a human being in himself," Holloway, *op. cit.*, p. 687.

[36] *Ibid.*, p. 670; also, "Treating of him as he is in himself in his own rights," "To a Historian," in "Inscriptions."

[37] Holloway, *op. cit.*, p. 670.

[38] "To You," in "Birds of Passage."

[39] Holloway, *op. cit.*, p. 670.

[40] *Complete Writings*, Vol. VI, Part I, 31.

essence identical with the one supreme being, exists not as a mode or partial expression of the absolute, but as a self-complete entity. The individual in Vedanta, unlike in Hegel, is not merely a part of the whole, but the whole itself. Each individual is essentially the whole and nothing but the whole. The soul is the whole of brahman;[41] as such it is supreme and all in all, "have you thought there could be but a single supreme?" Whitman asks. "There can be any number of supremes—one does not countervail another any more than one eyesight countervails another."[42] Whitman cannot accept the supremacy of one individual over another, or of the aggregate over the members. It is his profoundest conviction that all men are equally unique and supreme, and "all just as immortal and fathomless as myself."[43] Every portion of the universe is a microcosm, containing within itself the nature and meaning of the entire, all-inclusive macrocosm. The soul of the individual is identical with the soul of the world and contains all that the larger soul contains. "The central identity enables any one symbol to express successively all the qualities and shades of real being. In the transmission of divine waters, every hose fits every hydrant."[44]

This is not to say that individuals are quite separate from each other or that one soul is different from another. To affirm the uniqueness of individuals is not to deny their oneness. The individual souls are not a multitude of "windowless monads" shut up within their own concaves, yet bound together by an extraneous mechanical contrivance. At the core of his being the individual is one with the rest of the universe. The inner immortal self and the great cosmic power are one and the same.[45] Whitman, too, recognizes this:

> ... in respect to the Absolute soul, there is in the possession of such by each single individual, something so transcendent, so incapable of gradations (like life), that, to that extent, it places all being on a common level, utterly regardless of the distinctions of intellect, virtue, station.[46]

It is true that though individuals are different phenomenally, they are the same noumenally. At the noumenal level the soul loses its *jiva*

[41] *jīvō brahmaiva nāparah.*
[42] "By Blue Ontario's Shore," 3.
[43] "Song of Myself," 7.
[44] Emerson, "Swedenborg," *Representative Men.*
[45] See Brihadaranyaka, 3.4, *ēṣa ta ātmā sarvāntarah*, "This is your self which is within all."
[46] Holloway, *op. cit.,* p. 676.

appearance and becomes identical with *brahman,* one without a second. Yet for this very reason it is unique and therefore individual.[47] Individualism and universality are not mutually exclusive. They are in a sense one. Hence, Whitman sings of both separatism and en masse in one and the same breath. A "simple, separate person," yet he "utters the word Democratic, the word En-masse,"[48] because "every atom belonging to me, as good belongs to you."[49]

Whitman's name has been linked with Maritain, who popularized the term "personalism"[50] to designate a philosophy that "makes personality or selfhood the key to all reality." To Whitman, of course, the self is the key to all experience. But his own conception of selfhood or "personalism" is to be distinguished from a brand of philosophy known as "personalistic metaphysics."[51] The basic postulates of this philosophy are a dualistic epistemology that provides for all experienceable diversity, its acceptance of the empirical criteria, and its conception of a plurality or society of other selves or persons. Obviously, such a metaphysics is different from Whitman's mystical monistic conception. Whitman's universe is not a society of "pluralistic" selves, but an order based on the mystical perception of the "identified soul." Whitman's formula for reconciling the two mutually contradictory concepts of "completeness in separatism" and the aggregate is the idea of "personalism"[52]—which fuses the two. This personalism in Whitman's meaning is no other than the principle of the unitary self. The ground for the fusion of the two concepts is to be looked for in the "perfect uncontamination and solitariness of individuality," in which alone is the true "spirituality of religion." Thus, the clash between the individual and the universe, which belongs only to the surface level of one's consciousness, is resolved at the deeper level of the individual's own inner nature.

In Hegel's conception, the state, being the embodiment of the absolute, the existent divine idea, is the completion of the process of

[47] See P. T. Raju, *Thought and Reality: Hegelianism and Advaita* (London: George Allen, 1937), p. 62. Thus, in Vedanta the individual is saved both in his phenomenal and noumenal aspects.

[48] "One's-Self I Sing," in "Inscriptions."

[49] "Song of Myself," 1.

[50] See *Whitman Handbook.*

[51] See E. S. Brightman, "Personalist Metaphysics of the Self," in *Radhakrishnan: Comparative Studies in Philosophy* (London: George Allen & Unwin, 1951).

[52] "Personalism fuses this . . .," Holloway, *op. cit.,* p. 693.

world reason and as such an end in itself, not a means to anything. It is the final consummation through which the individual realizes his true life. The state is the true individual; and it is only by being a member in it, and by identifying his ends with its higher ends, that the individual realizes his individuality. Thus, what little spiritual reality the human being possesses is his only through the state. A doctrine such as this, which negates the individual, would be repugnant to the Vedantist and to an ardent individualist like Whitman. The state cannot be an end, good per se, unless it is a superperson, which Russel calls a "metaphysical monstrosity"; it is only a means. Its value is derived from the value of its members. It is not the aggregate that determines the individuals, but the individuals that "give character" to the aggregate. In the words of Whitman, "This idea of perfect individualism it is indeed that deepest tinges and gives character to the idea of the aggregate. For it is mainly or altogether to serve the independent separatism that we favor a strong generalization, consolidation."[53] In the final analysis, it is for the individual that the state exists, and in him does it realize its concreteness. "All is for individuals."[54]

> I swear I begin to see the meaning of these things,
> It is not the earth, it is not America who is so great,
> It is I who am great, or to be great, it is You up there, or any one,
> It is to walk rapidly through civilizations, governments, theories,
> Through poems, pageants, shows, to form individuals.
>
> Underneath all, individuals,
> I swear nothing is good to me now that ignores individuals,
> The American compact is altogether with individuals,
> The only government is that which makes minute of individuals,
> The whole theory of the universe is directed unerringly to one single
> individual—namely to You.[55]

It is for the self that all things are dear.[56] Civilizations, governments, theories, poems, pageants, shows—the purpose of all is to "form individuals." All the universes minister to the soul.[57] The ultimate

[53] *Ibid.*, p. 670.
[54] "By Blue Ontario's Shore," 3.
[55] *Ibid.*, 15.
[56] See Brihadaranyaka, 2.4.5. Yajnavalkya says to Maitreyi: *ātmanastu kāmaya sarvam priyam bhavati.* "It is for the sake of the self that all is loved."
[57] *Complete Writings*, Vol. VI, Part II, No. 175.

purpose of democracy or any state or government is to protect and cultivate the highest spiritual values found in the individual soul, "to develop, to open up to cultivation, to encourage the possibilities of all beneficent and manly outcroppage, and of that aspiration for independence and pride and self-respect latent in all characters." [58] It is for the purpose of raising the spiritual level of what he calls the "divine average" that Whitman favors government at all.[59] Whitman's aim is the "building up of the masses" by "building up grand individuals." "While the ambitious thought of my song is to help the forming of the great aggregate Nation, it is, perhaps, altogether through the forming of myriads of fully developed and enclosing individuals." [60] For he realizes that "so long as the spirit is not changed, any change of appearance is of no avail." [61] Again, "To lands, man, to woman, what is there at last to each, the inherent soul, nativity, idiocracy, free, high-poised, soaring its own flight, following out itself?" [62] It is finally in the individual soul rather than in the abstraction called the aggregate that spiritual values are realized at all. So Whitman says, "only in the perfect uncontamination and solitariness of individuality may the spirituality of religion positively come forth at all." Individuality favors the growth of spirituality; in religion individualism is more true. Hence do the Upanishads insist on the cultivation of inwardness, for religion is not essentially a social phenomenon but a personal experience. Religion is the functioning of the inward spirit. So the Upanishads proclaim, "The Self alone is to be meditated upon." [63] "Wisdom is of the soul," as Whitman points out, "wisdom cannot be passed from one having it to another not having it." [64] The same thought is also the purport of Emerson's conception in "Self-Reliance"

[58] Holloway, *op. cit.*, p. 675.

[59] Whitman's democracy ultimately ends in a kind of religious anarchism. The purpose of democracy is to train the individual man to become a law unto himself, to "train communities through all their grades to rule themselves." See Holloway, *op. cit.*, pp. 671, 675, 677. Contrast Hegel's belief that constitutional monarchy is the highest form of state, and its establishment the goal of history. Whitman, of course, does not preach lawlessness, even as no anarchist does. On the other hand, he allows that authority may continue till the individuals become fit for self-government.

[60] Holloway, *op. cit.*, p. 870.

[61] *Ibid.*, p. 706.

[62] *Ibid.*

[63] Brihadaranyaka, 1.4.7, *ātmētyēvōpāsīta*.

[64] "Song of the Open Road," 6.

and Whitman's statement that each man must travel the road for himself.[65]

> Alone, and silent thought and awe, and aspiration—and then the interior consciousness, like a hitherto unseen inscription, in magic ink, beams out its wondrous lines to the sense. Bibles may convey, and priests may expound, but it is exclusively for the noiseless operation of one's isolated Self, to enter the pure ether of veneration, reach the divine levels, and commune with the unutterable.[66]

Hegel, in his worship of the community, denies internality to the individual.[67] The individual in Hegel has no interior, only exterior; he has no "centripetal isolation" in Whitman's phrase. But man's nature cannot be interpreted in terms of his external setting. For what, viewed in his own right, is man but that "primal and interior something, in his soul's abysms, coloring all, and, by exceptional fruitions, giving the last majesty to him. . . ."[68] Hegel's excessive devotion to the god-state leads him to think that man's ultimate destiny is society and that salvation for him is possible only through it. The "everyman" (*Weltgeist*) of "phenomenology" transmigrating through the successive stages of dialectical progress returns at last to the social world and finds refuge in it. Religion Hegel regards as a "form of social consciousness."[69] Religion as a purely internal experience he dismisses as a mere phantasy, or a form of "unhappy consciousness." The Hindu view insists on the internality and the individualistic character of religion. Religion, according to it, is an inward realization, a growth from within. Man's true and essential greatness is individual. The self "socialized" is the self alienated from its own. Whitman asserts: "The ripeness of Religion is doubtless to be looked for in this field of individuality, and is a result that no organization or church can ever achieve. . . . Religion . . . is a part of the identified soul. . . ."[70]

[65] "Not I, not anyone else can travel that road for you, / You must travel it for yourself," "Song of Myself," 46.

[66] Holloway, *op. cit.*, p. 693.

[67] P. T. Raju, "The Inwardness of Indian Philosophy," *The Vedanta Kesari*, XXXIV, No. 7 (November 1947), 260–68.

[68] Holloway, *op. cit.*, p. 870.

[69] Josiah Royce, *Lectures on Modern Idealism* (New Haven: Yale University Press, 1919), p. 209.

[70] Holloway, *op. cit.*, p. 693.

For this very reason do both Emerson and Whitman express suspicion of all organized religion, in fact of all organized activity. Emerson felt that historical Christianity, by its insistence on the historical revelation of Christ and faith in his mediation, developed an external attitude toward religion. He recorded his dissatisfaction with it in his "Divinity School Address":

> In this point of view we become very sensible of the first defect of historical Christianity. Historical Christianity has fallen into the error that corrupts all attempts to communicate religion. As it appears to us, and as it has appeared for ages, it is not the doctrine of the soul but an exaggeration of the personal, the positive, the ritual. It has dwelt, it dwells, with noxious exaggeration about the person of Jesus.

Emerson complained that the vice of Swedenborg's mind was its "pernicious theologic limitation."[71] Both Swedenborg and Behmen failed by "attaching themselves to the Christian symbol." Whitman, too, felt the same dissatisfaction with the old Christian theology and founded his new democratic religion on the pride and infinitude of the private man.

> The whole scene shifts—the relative positions change—Man comes forward inherent, superb, the soul, the judge, the common average man advances, ascends to place. God disappears—the whole idea of God, as hitherto presented in the religions of the world for the thousands of past years . . . for reasons disappears—God abdicates.[72]

The Christian theological religion would not meet the demands of the "developed soul," whose original place is far above the conception of a personal deity. Therefore, the transcendentalists felt the need for a new impersonal doctrine, a "doctrine of the soul"—a religion which sought redemption, not in the church, but in the soul. "The remedy is already declared in the ground of our complaint of the Church. We have contrasted the Church with the soul. In the soul, then, let the redemption be sought."[73]

[71] "Swedenborg," *Representative Men.*
[72] *Whitman's Workshop*, pp. 43–44. Whitman also disapproves of the predominantly ethical attitude of the "Christian Cultus" with its distinction of right and wrong, "the bloodless cast-iron virtue," "Jaunt Calvinism." See *Complete Writings*, Vol. VI, Part II, No. 175.
[73] "Divinity School Address."

# CHAPTER SIX

# The Self and Reality

"I accept Reality and dare not question it,
. . . . . . .
Your facts are useful, and yet they are not my dwelling,
I but enter them to an area of my dwelling"

("Song of Myself," 23)

"What is I believe called Idealism seems to me to suggest . . . the course of inquiry and desert of favor for our New World metaphysics. . . ."[1] Such a belief in a type of idealism, which in Whitman's view should form the base of New World metaphysics, is also the sum and substance of his poetic thought. This belief was, of course, not a rationally formulated one, but one that was realized and expressed in poetic terms. However, there is in Whitman's poetry a unity and consistency of thought that lends itself to an analytical description. Whitman's idealism is essentially a mystical sort and in some important respects contrasts very sharply with the German dialectical doctrines which we have discussed earlier. Although, as is well known, Whitman spoke of Hegel in very enthusiastic terms, he was well aware of the shortcomings of Hegelian philosophy. The following is a frank admission from Whitman, expressing his dissatisfaction with Hegelianism:

> Nor does the Hegelian system strictly speaking explain the universe, either in the aggregate or in detail: The sense, the eyesight, life, the least insect, growth, the dynamics of nature are not eclaircised. Thought is not caught, held, dissected. To penetrate Nature and solve her problems the human faculties under present conditions are no more eligible now than before and under mortal conditions will in all probability never be eligible. The Eternal Mystery is still a mystery.[2]

Hegel and the post-Kantian idealists claimed that they explained the

[1] "Democratic Vistas," *Complete Poetry and Selected Prose and Letters*, edited by Emory Holloway (London: Nonesuch Press, 1938), pp. 712–13.
[2] *Complete Writings of Walt Whitman* (New York: G. P. Putnam's Sons, 1902), Vol. VI, Part II, No. 175.

universe rationally. But to Whitman the fact of life itself, the mystery and immensity of being, is beyond analysis and dissection.

> Compared to the vast oceanic volume of the unknown spiritual facts, what is all our own material knowledge before the immensity of that which is to come, the spiritual, the unknown, the immensity of being and facts around us of which we cannot possibly take any cognizance.[3]

Whitman's mystical, intuitional world stands in sharp contrast to Hegel's logical inferential realm. Here Kant's philosophy, with its conception of a noumenal reality, would be more in accord with Whitman's essentially mystical nature.

Nor does dialectic solve the fundamental metaphysical problem of finding a "fusing explanation and tie" between the me and the not-me. German idealism, no doubt, attempts to answer this question by saying that the objective world is the manifestation of the spirit or "creative thought." But as is implied in the very nature of dialectics, the actual existent world is posited as the antithesis of the spirit. Thus, dialectic, which is the spirit of Hegel's philosophy, cannot dispense with opposition, as opposition is the motive force of the whole process. This sense of resistance is no less prominent in Fichte, who conceives the physical world as the material for man's moral striving. In striking contrast to this is Whitman's conception of the spiritual identity of man and nature. Whitman never expresses the view that the world is an obstacle to be subdued; his writings are remarkably free from the sense of opposition and conquest. Whitman approaches nature not in a spirit of conquest but in an attitude of communion and mystical identification. "Specimen Days" and "Timber Creek" notes on nature reflect this unique attitude of oneness with nature—which is but an emotional equivalent of the sense of spiritual oneness, following directly on the emergence of the transcendental self. It is by such a mystical interpenetration of the self with all life and objects that Whitman is able to realize that "Objects gross and unseen soul are one." Schelling, no doubt, of the Germans, laid clear emphasis on the essential oneness of man and nature. In his philosophy nature is not regarded as being merely an obstacle or non-ego to be overcome, but it is regarded as intelligence striving toward consciousness. But even Schelling does not escape from the sense of dialectical conflict, for he regards nature

[3] Clifton Joseph Furness, *Walt Whitman's Workshop* (Cambridge: Harvard University Press, 1928), p. 40.

as a process of unconscious dialectic, evolving through the laws of polarity. Such a conception is, doubtless, foreign to Whitman. Nor does Schelling's idea that nature appears as a series of levels or gradations, each level differing from others in the degree of consciousness though in essence the same, seem to fit with Whitman's conception of the universe. Whitman does not seem to recognize any such hierarchy of forms or organisms. To him every individual existent object of the universe is, as it is, infinite.[4] "All the things of the universe are perfect miracles, each as profound as any."[5] In his attitude of spiritual equalitarianism he perceives, "a leaf of grass is no less than a journeywork of the stars, / And the pismire is equally perfect, and a grain of sand, and the egg of the wren."[6] The things of objective nature do not depend on an antithetical relation to one another but are united by a "divine rapport;" love is the foundation of the whole universal creation, "And that a Kelson of the creation is love."[7] Much in the same spirit the poet in the Upanishads sings that This earth is honey for all beings, and all beings are honey for this earth; this soul is honey for all things and all things are honey for this soul. Water, fire, air, sun, moon, sky, lightening etc. are all like honey for all beings and all beings are honey for them.[8]

What attracts Whitman in idealistic metaphysics is the importance and centrality it gives to the human self. Whitman also seems to have a fascination with the fundamental epistemological assumption of idealism that the world is in some sense unreal or non-ultimate, and that it is the creation of mind or self. To Whitman, the self being the ultimate reality, it alone confers upon objects their value and significance.[9] He even expresses the feeling that the world of objects may

[4] The "great chain of being" concept does not fully explain Whitman's philosophy. See Gay Wilson Allen, *Walt Whitman Handbook* (New York: Hendricks House, Inc., 1957), pp. 282–91. Also, for an excellent exposition of this concept see Arthur Lovejoy, *The Great Chain of Being* (Cambridge: Harvard University Press, 1936).

[5] "Starting from Paumanok," 12.

[6] "Song of Myself," 31.

[7] "Song of Myself," 5.

[8] Brihadaranyaka, 2.5.1–14.

[9] "The significant wonders of heaven and earth (significant only because of the Me in the centre)," "Democratic Vistas," Holloway, *op. cit.*, p. 689; ". . . the other pervading invisible fact . . . of life here . . . furnishing . . . the only permanent and unitary meaning to all," *ibid.*, pp. 729, f.; see also *ibid.*, pp. 698, 699, 734, 866.

have no existence except in the self of man. "What is the universe?
who knows? Maybe created by us, by winking of our eyes—preparing
us, by giving us identity—through the apparent known to the really
great unknown."[10]

> No one can realize any thing unless he has it in him ... or has been it.
> It must certainly tally with what is in him. ... Otherwise it is all blank
> to him. The animals, the past, light, space—if I have them not in
> me, I have them not at all. The future is in me as a seed or nascent
> thought.[11]

The goal of subject-object unity can be reached only by means of
epistemological idealism; and hence, all idealistic philosophies attempt
to solve the riddle of the self and the not-self by postulating that the
object is no more than the thought product of the self. Fichte derives
the world from the ego—which is not the subjective individual but
the universal ego transcending the limits of the subjective psychological
self. Schelling postulates an absolute world ground from which are
derived both nature and spirit. Vedanta, too, adopts the same standpoint and says that the manifold world is the projection of the absolute
self.[12] But post-Kantian epistemology, on the whole, inclines to a view
which denies reality to objects and regards them as ideas or apparitions.[13] The extreme idealism of Hegel asserts that the existing object
is nothing but a conflux of ideas or universals. Even Fichte is, to some
extent, guilty of this charge, since, in abandoning the things in themselves and treating them as but thoughts in the ego, he denied the
realistic element which is an essential ingredient of all knowledge.
Kant only, of the Germans, recognized the realistic element in knowledge, though he too held that the given thing-in-itself is invariably
colored and distorted in the knowing process. Whitman could never
have accepted the position of the Hegelian idealists. He, no doubt,
felt, as a result of the inner expansion, that the whole cosmic existence
is contained within his self, but he did not, for a moment, seem to

[10] Furness, *op. cit.*, p. 167.

[11] *Ibid.*, p. 46.

[12] The self is described in the Upanishads as creator. See Brihadaranyaka,
4.3.9, 10, 13; Chhandogya, 8.12.4, 5.

[13] According to Santayana this view is representative of the general character of
German idealism. See *Egotism in German Philosophy* (New York: Charles
Scribner's Sons, 1916).

doubt the existence of external objects. Beneath all his mysticism is a strong undercurrent of realism. Realism is the basis of Whitman's philosophical thinking; it is the bedrock of the American transcendentalism.

In respect to this fundamental metaphysical position Whitman comes nearest to the Vedantic idealists.[14] Whereas Hegel's doctrine, by identifying thought and thing, reduces the world to no more than a conflux of pure abstractions, Vedanta has a realistic epistemology. In the Vedanta, as in Kant, the knowing function does not create the object; knowledge is of the given. The object does not depend for its existence upon the subject but has an existence independent and complete in all respects. The function of knowledge is but to discover and reveal the existent thing-in-itself. The world is not mere categories, but it has an objective existence. However, what Vedanta tries to refute is the notion that finite objects have a reality apart from their substratum, the infinite *brahman*, which is the only real. The world is real, that is, it has existence, but it is not ultimate, that is, it has no existence independent of *brahman*. The doctrine of *maya*[15] does not make out that the world is non-existent, that it is an unreal phantasmagoria. Nowhere do the Upanishads suggest that the external world and the individual psychological selves are absolutely false. What is denied is not the reality of the world but its ultimacy. "Identity is non-difference; the world is non-existent apart from Brahman."[16] Finite things have only a relative reality, that is, apart from the absolute ground they are unreal. They are unreal also in the sense that they are not separate and self-subsistent. They exist as the non-dual *brahman*. The existence of the phenomenal is borrowed from the existence of the ideal. The belief that the finite is self-existent is due to *maya* or delusion. Sankara makes the Vedantic position clear when he says, "This whole

[14] For an excellent interpretation of Vedantic idealism, see P. T. Raju, *Thought and Reality: Hegelianism and Advaita* (London: George Allen, 1937), Part III.

[15] For an interpretation of the conception of *maya*, see Sarvepalli Radhakrishnan, *The Philosophy of the Upanishads* (London: George Allen & Unwin, 1935), pp. 57–74; *Eastern Religions and Western Thought* (London: Oxford University Press, 1940), pp. 31–32; Max Muller, *Three Lectures on the Vedanta Philosophy*, in *Collected Works of Max Muller* (London: Longman's Green & Co., 1901), XVI, 128–31.

[16] *ananyatvam vyatirēkēna abhāvah*; *brahmavyatirēkēna jagatō abhāvah*. Sankara's commentary on Brahma Sutra, II, i, 14.

multiplicity of production existing under name and form in so far as it is being itself is true. Of itself it is untrue." [17] The Upanishad describes the *brahman* as "real of the real." "Verily the breathing creatures are the Real. He is their Real." [18] "All these creatures·have their root in Being, they reside in Being, and rest in Being." [19]

Vedanta thus recognizes two planes of existence, or rather two standards of evaluation, the one relative, the other absolute, the one phenomenal, and the other metaphysical. Temporal existence is not false; it is not anybody's conception. But by itself it has no absolute reality. Name and form are valid empirically, but illusory when judged by absolute standards. The world has an empirical, but not metaphysical, validity. When it is asserted that the phenomenal is ephemeral, what is meant is not that it is non-existent, but that it finally disappears into the ideal. The idealism of the Vedanta is not, like that of Hegel, an idealism of ideas, but an idealism of the ideal. [20] It asserts that the ideal is the only real, that it is itself existence and actuality. There is thus in the Vedenta a realistic core which often escapes the notice of western readers. Vedanta, while it holds up the absolute as the ideal, does not deny all validity to the empirical world nor negate it absolutely but makes due allowance for it.

Whitman's devotion to realism, which is part of his temperament, dates back to the inception of *Leaves of Grass*. Here is one of the earliest formulations of his credo:

> I am the poet of reality,
> I say the earth is not an echo,
> Nor man an apparition;
> But all the things seen are real,
> The witness and albic dawn of things real
> And the world is no joke,
> Nor any part of it a sham. [21]

Whitman's interest in the concrete existential objects of the universe and his pantheistic reverence for the manifestations of nature disinclines

[17] Sankara's commentary on Chhandogya, 6.3.2.
[18] *satyasya satyam*, Brihadaranyaka, 2.3.6.
[19] Chhandogya, 6.8.6.
[20] See P. T. Raju, *op. cit.*, p. 257.
[21] Emory Holloway, *Uncollected Poetry and Prose* (New York: Doubleday, Doran & Co., 1922), I, 69–70.

him to the view which treats them as "bloodless categories." Time and again Whitman reiterates the conviction that the world is not a sham but is substantial and real.

> The domestic joys, the daily house work or business, the building of
> 　　houses, are not phantasms, they have weight, form, location,
> Farms, profits, crops, markets, wages, government, are none of them
> 　　phantasms,
>
> .　　.　　.　　.　　.　　.　　.　　.　　.
>
> The earth is not an echo, man and his life and all the things of his life
> 　　are well-consider'd.[22]

Whitman believes that the "object has a reality in itself"—independent of the knowing individual.[23] He does not suggest anywhere that objects have no existence apart from the knower. Whitman cannot concur with Fichte when he says that things are but thoughts in the ego, nor with Hegel when he says that the object is nothing but an idea. When, however, Whitman indicates idealism as the proper guide for New World metaphysics,[24] he does not understand by it idealism of the German type—which he would consider extravagant. The type of idealism Whitman envisages is of a mystical, transcendental brand, in which "the religious tone, the consciousness of mystery, the recognition of the future, of the unknown, of Deity over and under all, and of the divine purpose, are never absent," of which the unknown spiritual world is an essential ingredient. Such an idealism, according to Whitman serves as a counterpoise to "the growing excess and arrogance of realism," the modern worship of facts; it will rise above the visible material nature to "superior and spiritual points of view," and indicate that man's destination is "beyond the ostensible, the mortal."[25] For Whitman spirit is the foundation of the world, and as such it alone bestows reality on the world. The visible universe is rooted in the invisible; spirituality underlies all existence: "... the pervading invisible fact of life here ... furnishing ... the only

[22] "To Think of Time," 6. According to Hegel, objects being but categories or non-sensuous universals have neither "weight" nor "form" nor "location." They have no "existence," only logical reality. Vedanta does not accept this position.

[23] *Whitman's Workshop*, n. 138; also "Song of the Open Road," 6.

[24] Holloway, *op. cit.*, p. 713.

[25] *Ibid.*, p. 712.

permanent and unitary meaning to all." [26] When he declares that the unseen soul is "the real real, / (Purport of all these apparitions of the real)," [27] Whitman echoes faithfully the Upanishadic utterance which describes *brahman* as "real of the real" and avers that all creatures have their root in the *sat* (being). Emerson, too, claims that "the foundations of man are not in matter but in spirit." [28]

But though Whitman emphasizes that "the unseen soul" governs "absolutely at last," [29] he is far from allowing himself to lose sight of facts. "True, we must not condemn the show," he says, "neither absolutely deny it." [30] When, however, he states that "the conventional theories of life, worldly ambition, wealth, office, fame, etc., are essentially but glittering mayas, delusions," [31] that "the cry of sense, science, flesh, incomes, farms, merchandise, logic, intellect, demonstrations, solid perpetuities, buildings of brick and iron, or even the facts of the shows of trees, earth, rocks, etc.," are "illusions! apparitions! figments all!" [32] Whitman is not, as he himself admits, absolutely denying reality to them. What he denies is not the world's reality but its ultimate value. It is a judgment not so much from the standpoint of epistemology as from that of value. However, Whitman indicates, like the Vedantist, that, though the world is valuable for the "indispensability of its meanings" (that is empirically), for the "envision'd soul" who has attained to the superior spiritual point of view it woud "fall apart and vanish." [33] It would cease to have any significance. Thus, in so accepting the reality of the world and allowing for it its share of importance and validity and in emphasizing that the world, being but the reflection of the spirit, has no absolute value but only points to what is beyond itself, Whitman is in perfect accord with the Vedantist. Whitman's idealism, as also the Vedantist's, is more correctly characterized as mystical or *transcendental realism*.

[26] *Ibid.*, pp. 729, f.; also, "Wisdom is of the soul. . . . Is the certainty of the reality and immortality of things," "Song of the Open Road," 6.
[27] "Thou Mother with Thy Equal Brood," 6.
[28] "Nature."
[29] Holloway, *op. cit.*, p. 729.
[30] *Ibid.*, p. 713.
[31] *Complete Writings*, III, 271–72.
[32] Holloway, *op. cit.*, p. 713.
[33] *Ibid.*

Whitman, like a true Vedantist, denies ultimacy to the world. Beyond the ostensible Whitman recognizes the vast spiritual realm, which is the "real real." This eternal life is man's true destination, and the material world of shows is at best of an instrumental and pragmatic value. It is valued not for its own sake but for the "indispensability of its meanings"—as leading up to and preparing for "the eternal real life to come," [34] "the life that does not exhibit itself, yet contains all the rest." [35]

> The fact that concealed beneath the ostensible life which is celebrated in forms, politics, society, conversation, the churches and what is called knowledge and amusement, is the deep silent mysterious never to be examined . . . to which all those ostensible things ceaseless tending, the eternal life. . . . [36]

Hence, he says: "I sing the unaccomplished—I sing the vast dark unknown . . . Then chant (celebrate) the unknown, the future hidden spiritual world the real reality." [37] As the reality of the world is a derivative reality but not an ultimate reality, the human soul cannot anchor in it but rises through it to what is beyond it. This thought, that the physical universe is but a preparation for and an opening to the higher infinite existence and beatitude, is the keynote of Whitman's poems. "What is this universe? who knows? May be created by us, by winking of our eyes—preparing us, by giving us identity—through the apparent known, to the really great unknown." [38] The purpose of the finite, transient life is to lead the way to the unknown, eternal one. Finite objects are aids to spiritual realization and are of immense value for the spiritual aspirant, though they may be of no significance for the enlightened individual. The Hindu scriptures present the world as a seat of spiritual liberation. [39] It is a seat of spiritual evolution, where out of the material grows divine consciousness, out of the temporal, the immortal. So Whitman says:

> And I have dreamed that the purpose and essence of the known life,
>     the transient,

[34] "Song of Exposition," 7.
[35] "In Paths Untrodden," in "Calamus."
[36] *Whitman's Workshop*, p. 39.
[37] *Ibid.*, n. 14.
[38] *Ibid.*, p. 167.
[39] *mōkṣāyate samsārah.*

Is to form and decide identity for the unknown life, the permanent.
. . . . . . . . . .

I swear I think there is nothing but immortality,
That the exquisite scheme is for it, and the nebulous float is for it,
    and the cohering is for it!
And all preparation is for it—and identity is for it—and life and mater-
    ials are altogether for it![40]

Spirituality is the culmination of the world process,[41] and as such
the only ultimate value. Material objects are "appearances," no doubt,
when viewed in the light of the ultimate, but they should not on that
score be repudiated, as they are in themselves revealing. Finite objects
help us to realize the infinite.[42] *Maya* itself is a means to salvation, and,
as Whitman says, "You furnish your parts toward eternity, / Great
or small, you furnish your parts toward the soul."[43] Science, ships,
politics, cities, factories are not nothing; they are solid things, they
stand for realities. But higher than these is the spiritual world which is
the real reality.[44] Whitman, like the Vedantic idealist, accords to the
world only a lesser kind of reality—a relative reality. He does not, again
like the Vedantist, absolutely deny it value or existence. He accepts
reality and dares not question it.[45] To materialism and positive science
he accords "first honors" but warns us in the same breath that it must
not be supposed that these are his dwelling. "Your facts are useful,"
he admits, "and yet they are not my dwelling, / I but enter by them to
an area of my dwelling."[46]

In so treating the world as having only an empirical reality or
pragmatic justification and holding up the soul or self as the only
ideal, Whitman offers a genuine case for what is termed "otherworldliness," which is a general characteristic of eastern religions, and of Hindu
religion pre-eminently.[47] Otherworldliness, on the Hindu view,

[40] "To Think of Time," 8, 9.
[41] "Spirituality . . . the finale of visible forms," "Starting from Paumanok," 5.
[42] See Sankara's commentary on Brihadaranyaka, 2.1.14.
[43] "Crossing Brooklyn Ferry," 9.
[44] See "As I Walk These Broad Majestic Days," in "From Noon to Starry Night."
[45] See "Song of Myself," 23.
[46] *Ibid.* See also "Starting from Paumanok," 8; and "one who does not condemn civilization and refinement but grows through them to be superior to them,"
*Complete Writings*, VI, Part I, 68.
[47] See Radhakrishnan, *Eastern Religions and Western Thought*, p. 75.

implies that the world we know here and now is not final and that the highest good can be sought only in a higher realm of being, which is spiritual. It does not, however, negate the world of the lower order and condemn it as absolutely false and worthless.[48] Otherworldliness, again, is not the belief in a future life, nor the desire for a prolongation of the joys and pleasures of terrestrial existence, with the omission of its painful features.[49] On the other hand it is the craving for release from the empirical existence, and for life on a higher plane of being. Maitreyi in the Brihadaranyaka (2.4) presents a typical instance of this attitude. Otherworldliness is the dominant attitude of the American transcendentalists. It is the keynote of Emerson. It is predominant in Thoreau, and constitutes the informing spirit of *Walden*. Otherworldliness pictures the worldly life as a preparation for the unseen spiritual existence. It is opposed to the attitude of humanism, namely, materialistic self-sufficiency. It asks us, "fix not thy heart on that which is transitory"[50] and says with Whitman, "they are not my dwelling."

Man's real habitat is the realm of eternal values. With our minds anchored in the infinite we have to strive in our actual lives to approximate the truths of the transcendental order. The Gita calls upon us to live our lives in a spirit of detachment and renunciation, our eyes fixed on the beyond. Yājñavalkya in the Brihadaranyaka impresses upon us that the objects of the world exist, and are loved, not for themselves as they appear but for the self that is in them, for the eternal they contain.[51] Echoing the Upanishadic saying, Whitman says, "Each is not for its own sake, / I say the whole earth and all the stars in the sky are for religion's sake."[52] The finite has only an instrumental value. The visible points to the invisible and culminates in it; "spirituality" is "the finale of visible forms."[53] And because the invisible is as real and definite as the visible,[54] the old seer passes the objects and hues of

[48] See *ibid.*, p. 64. "It is not correct to describe Indian mysticism as life-and-world-negating."

[49] See Lovejoy, *The Great Chain of Being*, pp. 24–26.

[50] Quoted in *Walden*, chap. i.

[51] Brihadaranyaka, 2.4.5, "Verily, a husband is not dear that you may love the husband, but that you may love the Self is a husband dear."

[52] "Starting from Paumanok," 7.

[53] *Ibid.*, 5.

[54] Holloway, *op. cit.*, p. 872.

the world "to glean eidólons," knowing "the ostent is evanescent."[55]

> I met a seer,
> Passing the hues and objects of the world,
> The fields of art and learning, pleasure, sense,
> To glean eidólons.

"What are those of the known but to ascend and enter the unknown? / And what are those of life but for Death?"[56] is a typical example of his otherworldliness.

The same attitude of renunciation and detachment forms the dominant spirit of "Song of the Open Road," in which Whitman depicts himself as a pilgrim and a wayfarer, and the universe itself as a road for traveling souls. In Section 9 the poet recognizes that the objects of the world are fugitive and refuses to be allured by them:

> Allons! we must not stop here,
> However sweet these laid-up stores, however convenient the dwelling
>     we cannot remain here,
> However sheltered this port and however calm these waters we must
>     not anchor here.

The wise man, knowing the fugitive nature of the world, passes beyond it to "that which is endless as it was beginningless." He, nevertheless, lives and acts in this world without passion or attachment, "enjoying all without labour or purchase, abstracting the feast yet not abstracting a particle of it."[57] The Upanishad asks us to enjoy by renouncing.[58] Echoing the Upanishadic saying, Thoreau writes, "Let not to get a living be thy trade, but thy sport. Enjoy the land but own it not."[59] The same thought inspires Emerson's poem "Hamatreya":

> Earth laughs in flowers, to see her boastful boys,
> Earth-proud, proud of the earth which is not theirs
>     Mine and yours
>     Mine, not yours.

[55] "Eidólons," in "Inscriptions."
[56] "Portals," in "Songs of Parting."
[57] "Song of the Open Road," 13.
[58] Isa, 1, *tyaktēna bhunjeetthāh.*
[59] *Walden,* chap. x.

The sense of the transiency of worldly things sometimes grows so strong upon him that Whitman doubts their reality even.

> Hast never come to thee an hour,
> A sudden gleam divine, precipitating, bursting all these bubbles, fashions, wealth?
> These eager business aims—books, politics, art, amours,
> To utter nothingness?[60]

For all his rapturous acceptance of the everyday and the earthly, Whitman is forever escaping and transcending it. For he realizes that material purposes do not ultimately satisfy the soul. Religion begins with renunciation. So long as men and women pass unwittingly "the true realities of life, and go toward false realities"[61]— positions, ceremonies, wealth, and the like—spirituality will remain at a distance. Hence it is that Whitman keeps insisting that an "all-penetrating Religiousness"[62] is the sole "verteber of" democracy and civilization[63] and that, without a force infusion making for spiritualization, modern civilization, with all its colossal achievements, should end in a fiasco. Science, technology, politics, even democracy are only means to inner development,[64] and the gravest danger to society lies in a possible overemphasis of the former to the exclusion of the latter.[65] Outward expansion and material aggrandizement are not the criteria for greatness of character, of a nation or of an individual. The main thing is "its own soul."[66] Democracy is valuable only insofar as it yields spiritual results. Whitman insists that a "great moral and religious civilization" is "the only justification of a great material one."[67] The humanistic standpoint of self-sufficient materialism disregards this essential element in life; for, in the final analysis, mortal

[60] "Hast Never Come to Thee an Hour," in "By the Roadside."

[61] "Thought," in "Autumn Rivulets."

[62] Holloway, *op. cit.*, p. 693.

[63] See "Democratic Vistas," *ibid.* Also, "I say the real and permanent grandeur of these states must be their religion, / Otherwise there is no real and permanent grandeur," "Starting from Paumanok," 7.

[64] See Holloway, *op. cit.*, p. 714, "As fuel to flame, and flame to heavens, so must wealth, science, materialism,—even this democracy of which we make so much—unerringly feed the highest mind, the soul;" also "Starting from Paumanok," 8.

[65] See Holloway, *op. cit.*, pp. 665–68.

[66] *Ibid.*, p. 572.

[67] *Ibid.*, p. 668.

life is important only with reference to the immortal, which is the only permanently real.[68] In thus giving religion primacy over all else and in stressing the importance of inner spiritual life, Whitman is more perfectly in accord with the spirit of the eastern rather than the western tradition of thought. The exclusive emphasis on religion and inner life as the chief ends of existence belongs to eastern religions pre-eminently. Humanism is the predominant feature of western thought.[69] The Greeks were humanistic thinkers essentially; their philosophy was rationalistic, their politics nationalistic.[70] German philosophy, especially, is humanistic to the core.

Whitman's faith in the perfection of all existent objects of the universe, and the prestige and uniqueness he bestows on individual human selves, divides him further from the German philosophers. The ethical activism of Fichte conceives a sharp contraposition between the self and the phenomenal world, empirical reality and ideal reality, and makes this conflict between them the motive principle of the self's progress. Schelling asserted that the processes of nature and the processes of the inner life of man are analogous, but his evolutionistic conception of the universe as a hierarchical order or an ascending scale of being not only derogates from the excellence and dignity of the existent individual as by itself complete and infinite but makes perfection not a realized fact but the flying goal of the whole of things. In Fichte, too, perfection is the unattainable goal of an endless process. Thus, there is here a schism between the real and the ideal, between existence and value. Not only does Whitman not conceive any such chasm between the real and the ideal,[71] but to him perfection is eternally realized in the present moment. This realization has, of course, come to him as a result of the self-knowledge wherein it is perceived that the transient individual and the everlasting one are identical. The individual, for realizing his true status, need not undertake, as the Germans would have him do, an endless task of advancing toward an ideal that shall never become actual. Every finite being is, as he is,

---

[68] *Ibid.*, p. 698; also "Life, life is the tillage, and Death is the harvest according," "As I Watched the Ploughman Ploughing," in "Whispers of Heavenly Death."

[69] See Radhakrishnan, *Eastern Religions and Western Thought*, p. 75.

[70] *Ibid.*, pp. 2–7.

[71] See F. O. Matthiessen, *American Renaissance* (New York: Oxford University Press, 1941), p. 519, "For Whitman there was no chasm between the real and the ideal."

immortal and limitless, "all just as immortal and fathomless as myself, / (They do not know how immortal, but I know.)."[72] Again, "Our immortality is located here upon earth—that we are immortal."[73]

Whitman sees eternal perfection; he sees everything existing always, everything accomplished in the eternal present:

> There was never any more inception than there is now,
> Nor any more youth or age than there is now,
> And will never be any more perfection than there is now,
> Nor any more heaven or hell than there is now.[74]

To Whitman the present moment has the deepest reality, for he has gained that being which is self-contained and eternal, and whose fulness and perfection nothing and no process can supplement or enhance. So he exists as he is, and that is enough for him.[75] "Other poets have formed for themselves an idea apart from positive life, and disdainful of it but for me I ask nothing better or more divine than real life, here, now, yourself, your work."[76] So Whitman loses himself in the immensity of the moment: "Each moment and whatever happens thrills me with joy."[77] Happiness is in the moment; it is not in the future. In the present moment is the consummation of our life. And, therefore, the poet is "satisfied with the present"[78] and exalts the present and the real.[79] This feeling of the depth and reality of the now is expressed in the following lines of Emerson: "But do I not know the Now to be the Eternal? . . . I believe in this life."[80]

It is this sense of eternity that inspires Whitman's total and unreserved acceptance of reality and his "unrestricted faith."[81] For to Whitman the real and the ideal are one; the existent fact is the ideal value.[82] Mystical intuition tends to the dissolution of dualities. In it

[72] "Song of Myself," 7.
[73] *Complete Writings*, Vol. VI, Part II, No. 144.
[74] "Song of Myself," 3.
[75] See *ibid.*, 20.
[76] *Complete Writings*, Vol. VI, Part I, No. 52.
[77] "Song of Myself," 24.
[78] Holloway, *op. cit.*, p. 583.
[79] "To exalt the present and the real," "Song of the Exposition," 7.
[80] Quoted in Matthiessen, *op. cit.*, p. 11.
[81] "I accept reality and dare not question it," "Song of Myself," 23.
[82] "The simple and the commonplace with him included the ideal and the spiritual," R. M. Bucke, *Cosmic Consciousness* (14th ed.; New York: E. P. Dutton & Co., Inc, 1948), p. 218.

the highest truths are seen as already accomplished in the actual. The Mahayana Buddhists identify nirvana and world order (*samsāra*).[83] The difference between truth and error does not exist; what men think is sin or delusion is itself intelligence.[84] Since the ideal is the only real, whatever is is ideal and real.[85] It is this realization that allows Whitman to pass by the ugliness and contradictions of the world in supreme indifference; he knows that they do not belong to the essence of things and that they are, in fact, a delusion. "Everything is beautiful in itself and perfect."[86]

Whitman's poetic materialism is rooted in his mystical approach to reality. The poet, according to Whitman is concerned with facts, not with fiction. History and poetry subserve the same function, and are more or less interchangeable terms; "the best poetry is the real history."[87] Nor does Whitman see any real antagonism between poetry and science. The message of the poet and the scientist is the same, that all objects are perfect.[88] Whitman accepts science because it gives confirmation to his intuitions by enjoining absolute acceptance of the universe. Hence, according to Whitman, poetry must be "consistent with modern science,"[89] and poets "will absorb whatever science indicates."[90] Whitman himself "imbues" materialism and makes the poems of materials, for "I think they are to be the most spiritual poems."[91]

Whitman shares Wordsworth's faith that there is for the poet no necessity "to trick out or to elevate"[92] the common scenes of nature. Instead the real task is to see them in their true light, to perceive and image forth the grandeur that belongs to every real thing and to real things only. This explains Whitman's antagonism to romances. "No dainty dolce affetuoso I,"[93] Whitman declares: "Great genius and the

---

[83] *yahklēsah sō bōdhi, yah samsārah tat nirvāṇam*, Nagarjuna.

[84] See "Transpositions."

[85] "What will be will be well, for what is is well," "To Think of Time," 6.

[86] Furness, *Whitman's Workshop*, p. 66.

[87] *Complete Writings*, Vol. VI, Part II, No. 24.

[88] Norman Foerster, *American Criticism* (Boston: Houghton Miffin Co., 1928), pp. 201–2.

[89] Holloway, *op. cit.*, p. 716.

[90] *Ibid.*, p. 717.

[91] "Starting from Paumanok," 6.

[92] See A. E. Morgan, *The Beginnings of Modern American Poetry* (London: Longmans, Green & Co., 1946), p. 5. The writer thinks that Whitman's poetic faith is rooted in the Wordsworthian philosophy.

people of these states must never be demean'd to romances. As soon as histories are properly told, no more need of romances." 94

While the English romantics all fled from the sordidness and squalor of city life, while Emerson shyed away to the country solitude, and Thoreau took shelter at Walden Pond, Whitman abandoned himself to sprawling New York in its iron age and sang songs for engines, trades, factories and occupations and found in them "eternal meanings." 95 Thus, in Whitman's view the task of poetry is not so much to idealize as to see things in their true colors. Whitman sets forth his creed of realistic art thus:

> In these "Leaves" *everything is literally photographed. Nothing is poetised*, no divergence, not a step, not an inch, nothing for beauty's sake, no euphemism, no rhyme. [But] an awful adherence to the truth.96

Consequently the supreme function of poetry is to cleave "through all interpositions and coverings and turmoils and stratagems to first principles." 97

> It is not a labor of clothing or putting on or describing—it is a labor of clearing away and reducing—for *everything is beautiful in itself and perfect* —and the office of the poet is to remove what stands in the way of one perceiving the beauty and perfection.98

It is Whitman's lack of the capacity for idealization that in Santayana's opinion makes him a poet of barbarism99—the capacity for an imaginative rendering of human life and its meaning. But Whitman has small use for idealization of that type. To him poetry is not make-believe; its function is not to "poetize" facts and throw upon them the glamor of illusion. Hence he sees in the locomotive and the multiplication table genuine themes for poetry. As Emerson says in "Nature,"

> We make fables to hide the baldness of the fact and conform it, as we say, to the higher law of the mind. But when the fact is seen under the light of an idea, the gaudy fable fades and shrivels. We behold the real

93 "Starting from Paumanok," 15.
94 Holloway, *op. cit.*, p. 581; also *Complete Writings*, Vol. VI, Part II, No. 66.
95 "A Song for Occupations," 1.
96 *Complete Writings*, Vol. VI, Part I, No. 88.
97 Holloway, *op. cit.*, p. 581.
98 *Whitman's Workshop*, p. 66. (Italics mine.)
99 "The Poetry of Barbarism," *Interpretations of Poetry and Religion* (New York: Charles Scribner's Sons, 1916).

higher law. To the wise, therefore, a fact is true poetry, and the most beautiful of fables.

Inconsistent as it may seem with these notions of eternity, perfection and infinitude, Whitman also speaks of development, cosmic evolution and progress in time. On the one hand he speaks of being, which is in the eternal moment and which involves no process in time. On the other hand he believes in "eternal progress";[100] he calls himself an evolutionist and speaks of the law of successions as the greatest law of nature.[101] He betrays a constant preoccupation with time and space, but at the same time he is not quite unaware of that eternity which is the bond of all time, that similitude which underlies the seemingly disparate.[102] Similarly, Whitman makes contradictory statements regarding evil. In one and the same breath he denies evil and insists that it is not a delusion. He does not see one imperfection in the universe,[103] but still he pins his faith to the future for the solution of all discrepancies, fears, and doubts, and says, "If the future is nothing they are just as surely nothing."[104]

Critics have tried to explain this discrepancy in Whitman, but the answer they have found to it is not satisfactory. Regarding the question of evil and Whitman's optimism critical opinion has generally inclined to the view that Whitman's optimism springs from his faith in cosmic melioration and social progress and that he justifies evil and imperfection by reference to the universal harmony.[105] The following sums up the position:

> Whitman's desire to be the poet of evil as well as that of good sprang not so much from his optimism (i.e., denial of the existence of evil) or his failure to observe pain, cruelty, oppression, etc., in the world he lived in as from his belief in cosmic and moral evolution.[106]

[100] "Starting from Paumanok," 2.

[101] "The law over all laws, and law of laws, is the law of successions; that of the superior law in time, gradually supplanting and overwhelming the inferior one," Holloway, *op. cit.*, p. 677; see also Norman Foerster, *op. cit.*, p. 202.

[102] See Holloway, *op. cit.*, p. 584.

[103] "Song at Sunset," in "Songs of Parting."

[104] "To Think of Time," 1.

[105] See Joseph Warren Beach, *The Concept of Nature in Nineteenth Century English Poetry* (New York: Macmillan Co., 1936), p. 389; *Wordsworthian and Other Studies* (Oxford: Clarendon Press, 1947); Allen, *Whitman Handbook*, p. 357.

[106] *Whitman Handbook*, p. 357.

Dorothy F. Mercer, whose comparative study of Whitman and the Gita is till now the only one of its kind, also attempts to explain this question. She says:

> Manifestly, it is not that Whitman does not see sin, disease, and death; but that he has seen them as parts of an harmonious becoming. . . . Sin, disease, death are each in their rightful place.[107]

> Whitman builds his house on the vision of a future utopia; he is content because he sees an eventual perfection. . . . (His) optimism does not depend upon a denial of evil but on an eventual annihilation of it through progressive evolution.[108]

It is true that Whitman sees evil, sin, and suffering; but it is equally patent that he denies them any significance or reality. Then there is the general discrepancy between the two utterly different points of view which Whitman's works present. Mercer's solution to this, if we may judge from her published articles, is rather ambiguous. A satisfactory solution can, however, be found only when we read these statements of Whitman in the light of the Vedanta, and give equal weight to all the statements made by him instead of emphasizing some and overlooking others, in which case our solution is bound to be one-sided.

Whitman's position in regard to this needs to be stated clearly before a synthetic interpretation can be attempted. Concerning evil, Whitman makes the following statement:

> Here is what sings unrestricted faith.

> Omnes! Omnes! let others ignore what they may,
> I make the poem of evil also, I commemorate that part also,
> I am myself just as much evil as good, and my nation is—and I say,
>     there is in fact no evil.[109]

and in a later section, he says, "And I will show that there is no imperfection in the present, and can be none in the future."[110] In "Song of Myself," 22 he claims "What blurt is this about virtue and about vice? /

---

[107] "Whitman on Prophecy," *Vedanta. and the West*, XI (July-August, 1948), 118–23.
[108] "Whitman on Reincarnation," *Vedanta and the West*, IX (November-December, 1946), 180–85.
[109] "Starting from Paumanok," 7.
[110] *Ibid.*, 12.

Evil propels me and the reform of evil propels me, I stand indifferent," and "What is called good is perfect, and what is called bad is just as perfect."[111] The following is no less explicit and decisive: "I am the poet of sin, / For I do not believe in sin."[112] But though Whitman thus denies the existence of evil and refuses to make moral distinctions, he is no less emphatic in declaring, "The difference between sin and goodness is no delusion."[113] Contrary to the statement that there is no imperfection in the present and there will be none in the future, he believes that we are all progressing as we should: "'We are all onward, onward, speeding slowly, surely bettering, / ... All bound as is befitting each—all surely going somewhere.'"[114] And he has also faith in the universal harmony: "The universe is duly in order, everything is in its place."[115] Whitman's faith in evolution, teleology, and cosmic meliorism on the one hand,[116] and his belief in eternal perfection on the other, together with the conviction that evil and imperfection are a lie and a mistake, apparently continue side by side. Neither the one nor the other of these two aspects can be left out of account in considering the poetic belief of Whitman.

Whitman seems to recognize two distinct planes of existence—the one phenomenal, the other metaphysical. He seems, in his evaluation of life, to view things from two different standpoints—from the point of view of the enlightened individual, and that of those who are unenlightened, and who live on the empirical level. And though he has himself gained the supreme salvation and is conscious of his own superiority, his concern for the salvation of others keeps him constantly thinking about them. Nevertheless, the distinction between him, the liberated soul, and others is constantly present to his mind.

> To think of all these wonders of city and country, and others taking
>     great interest in them, and we taking no interest in them.
> To think how eager we are in building our houses,
> To think others shall be just as eager, and we quite indifferent.[117]

[111] "To Think of Time," 8.
[112] Holloway, *op. cit.*, II, 71.
[113] "To Think of Time," 6.
[114] "Going Somewhere," in "Sands at Seventy."
[115] "Sleepers," 7.
[116] "That this earth is under a constant process of amelioration," *Complete Writings*, Vol. VI, Part II, No. 144.
[117] "To Think of Time," 8.

He knows that to those who have known the self ethical distinctions have no meaning, for such distinctions, being the result of ignorance, obtain only on the lower empirical plane. The values and standards of this world do not hold when the higher point of view is reached. Once metaphysical knowledge is gained, evil, sin, suffering, even *maya* itself, disappear. So Whitman says, "The vulgar and the refined, what you call sin and what you call goodness, to think how wide a difference, / To think the difference will still continue to others, yet we lie beyond the difference."[118] Knowing this he stands indifferent to both good and evil. While others discuss, he is silent. "Showing the best and dividing it from the worst age vexes age, / Knowing the perfect fitness and equanimity of things, while they discuss I am silent, and go bathe and admire myself."[119]

For, is not the world of *brahman* free from all evil?[120] Speaking as an "envision'd soul," he asserts that there is in fact no evil and that the "local considerations of sin, disease, deformity, ignorance, death" obtain only for the "superficial mind."[121] But Whitman is not blind to the existence of evil, sin, and failings—which constitute an inescapable fact in the world of phenomena, and which it would be foolish to deny or disregard. So when he says that "the difference between sin and goodness is no delusion," he only means that in the world of facts evil presents a problem and as such it is to be faced, and not treated with complacence. Whitman, thus, denies evil only from the point of view of knowledge, though from the point of view of ignorance he concedes that there is evil. Speaking from the higher standpoint, he says that

> Out of the bulk, the morbid and the shallow,
> Out of the bad majority, the varied countless frauds of men and states,

[118] *Ibid.*, 5. Also, "The living look upon the corpse with their eyesight, / But without eyesight lingers a different living and looks curiously on the corpse." (*Ibid.*, 2.) Here the suggestion is that there is a view of death at the physical, finite level, and there is also a truer "superior" view of it from the standpoint of the mind that has extricated itself from the circumstances of time and death, and looks on the time-process (birth and decay) with a detached interest or with a neutral attitude, "What will be will be well—for what is is well, / To take interest is well, and not to take interest shall be well." (*Ibid.*, 5.)

[119] "Song of Myself," 3.

[120] "For, this world of Brahman [*brahmalōka*] is free from all evils. All evils turn away from it," Chhandogya, 8.4.1.

[121] Holloway, *op. cit.*, pp. 713–14.,

Electric, antiseptic yet, cleaving, suffusing all,
Only the good is universal.[122]

And, therefore, his object would be "not to exclude or demarcate,
or pick out" evil but to "celebrate the immortal and the good."[123]
William James quotes Whitman as an example of healthy-mindedness,
which, according to him, consists in conceiving good as the essential
and universal aspect of being and deliberately excluding evil from its
field of vision. Healthy-mindedness "looks on all things and sees that
they are good."[124] Whitman realizes that evil, being but phenomenal,
does not possess metaphysical significance, and as such it cannot find
any place in his ultimate scheme of things.

Distinction must be made at this point between healthy-mindedness
of this type and the optimism that is generally attributed to the Hegelian
idealists. The attitude of Hegel with regard to evil is, in the words of
William James, "that everything actual is rational, and that evil, as an
element dialectically required, must be pinned in and kept consecrated
and have a function awarded to it in the final system of truth."[125]
"The world," as Bradley admirably sums it up, "is the best of all
possible worlds, and everything in it is a necessary evil." But though
Hegel says that contradictions are dialectically necessary, he would not
agree to call them evil. For, such a conclusion would be untenable on
the assumption that all reality is rational and righteous. However,
what makes the universe, which is completely rational, seem imperfectly
rational is, according to Hegel, the delusion of our own minds. "The
good, the absolutely good, is eternally accomplishing itself in the
world ... is already by implication as well as in full actuality accomplished"; but illusion makes it seem yet unaccomplished. Evil or
imperfection, then, is a delusion.[126] But this conclusion of Hegel is
incompatible with the facts because it pays no regard to the irrationality
and unrighteousness which are notoriously real in our everyday life.
What he denies in theory Hegel thus justifies in effect. Such an

---

[122] "Song of the Universal," 2, in "Birds of Passage."
[123] "L. of G.'s Purport," in "Good-Bye My Fancy."
[124] William James, *Varieties of Religious Experience* (New York: Modern
Library, 1936), p. 86.
[125] *Ibid.*, p. 130.
[126] See John McTaggart, *Studies in the Hegelian Dialectic* (Cambridge: University Press, 1922), Chapter: "The Relation of the Dialectic to Time."

unrealistic doctrine would be quite unacceptable in Whitman's view. To him evil is an undeniable fact of our daily experience. He would not, moreover, agree that contradictions are necessary, nor would he accept evil as part of reality. Imperfections, according to him, are unmeaning only when judged from the "superior and spiritual points of view."[127]

The Vedantic conception will be found to accord better with this position of Whitman in regard to evil. The Vedantic view does not deny the existence of evil but only denies that it touches the absolute. Evil belongs to the phenomenal world of *maya*; it has only epistemological existence. The root evil, according to Vedanta, is the metaphysical evil, that is, ignorance or *avidya*. So long as right knowledge is not acquired, evil persists. Vedanta thus recognizes two different points of view, the empirical and the absolute. The former standpoint provides for evolution and time process. Though the absolute is timeless and supra-dimensional, time and space are realities that govern the empirical existence. Whereas Hegel declares time and space to be appearances only,[128] and Kant treats them as merely categories of thought, the Vedanta accepts them as categories of existence,[129] while, of course, emphasizing that they ultimately vanish in the absolute. The general position of the Vedanta philosophy in regard to this is set forth in the Upanishads thus: "There are assuredly two forms of Brahman: the formed and the formless, the mortal and the immortal, the actual and the yon."[130] The one is spirit-in-transcendence, the other spirit-in-immanence. The former, the pure being or the modeless absolute, the other, the dynamic divine engaged in self-expression and creative activity. In the field of expression there is change and evolution, for expression implies concreteness and concentration. But this dynamic development of the *brahman* is not inconsistent with its essential nature as changeless being. For the absolute puts forth the world of forms while itself remaining unaffected.[131] It merely develops its indefinite possibilities, creates out of its superabundance. Creation, which means self-expression, cannot limit or exhaust the nature of

---

[127] Holloway, *op. cit.*, p. 713.
[128] See McTaggart, *op. cit.*, chap. v.
[129] I.e., they are independent of us.
[130] Brihadaranyaka, 2.3.1.
[131] This theory is known as *vivartavāda*.

the agent who expresses. The artist is not worked off in the process of art. Development or becoming, again, belongs to the field of expression only, not to that of knowing. Knowing is not a progressive act, but it is in the moment. It is being, not becoming. The Brahman intuited himself as "I am Brahman"[132] that is, in pure self-immediacy, and as a result of this self-knowledge became all. The presence of the created world does not, again, take away from the glory of the infinite.[133] There are thus two orders of being, the higher and the lower (*pāra-mārthika satta, vyāvahārika satta*). The lower, the name and form world, does not contradict the higher—the absolute reality but serves as a stepping stone to the higher. Name and form are used to reach the formless.[134] "From the point of view of metaphysics (*paramārtha*) no manifestation is to be taken as absolutely true, while from the standpoint of experience (*vyavahāra*) every one of them has some validity."[135]

Whitman's general position in regard to all outstanding metaphysical questions is much the same as that of the Vedanta. Whitman, like the Vedantist, seems to think that evil, progress, and the processes in time and space are significant only for the undeveloped individual and that the "developed soul" has an existence far above these empirical categories. He believes in evolution and accepts the reality of time and space, but he is aware that his own realized self has a being quite independent of the contingencies of worldly existence. While he knows that moral distinctions are invalid with reference to himself and that his soul is unaffected by the presence of evil and suffering in the world around him, he recognizes that evil has a reality to ordinary men; and

[132] Brihadaranyaka, 1.4.10; "Not the actual cognition of the self as an object," Sankara's commentary.

[133] The relation of the absolute to the creation is described in the famous Upanishadic verse: "The Whole is all that. The Whole is all this. The Whole is born out of the Whole. When the Whole is absorbed into the Whole the Whole alone remains;" See also Gita, 7.12.24; 9.4.5; 10.42; see Rene Guenon, *Man and His Becoming*, tr. by Richard C. Nicholson (London: Luzag & Co., 1945), pp. 29, 30, 55, 82, 83.

[134] "The knowledge of the conditioned Brahman leads to that of the supreme Brahman," Sankara's commentary on Brihadaranyaka, 2.1.14.

[135] Radhakrishnan, *The Bhagavad Gita* (London: George Allen & Unwin, Ltd., 1948). See editor's commentary on 4.11. *Maya* is not illusionism. It only denotes the onesidedness of the relation between the absolute and the world. "Maya is the principle of inexplicability." It denotes that no conceivable relation exists between the infinite and the finite forms. See P. T. Raju, *op. cit.*, pp. 31, 154.

it is for the amelioration of the world that Whitman sees that time and growth are necessary.

> Eternal trains of purpose, in the development, by however slow degrees, of the physical, moral, and spiritual kosmos.... Time and space, in the will of God, furnish successive chains, completions of material births and beginnings solve all discrepancies, fears, and doubts, and eventually fulfil happiness.[136]

When Mercer says that Whitman's optimism does not depend upon a denial of evil but on an eventual annihilation of it through progressive evolution and that Whitman builds his house on the vision of a future utopia, evidently, she bases her view on such statements of Whitman as the one above. But other statements, such as: "Happiness, knowledge, not in another place but this place, not for another hour but this hour," go to show that her conclusion is at best only partial.[137] To Whitman, speaking in reference to himself, happiness and perfection are not future events, depending on a gradual unfolding in time, but they are consummated even now. The poet lives in what is called eternal being and takes infinite delight in existence as such:

> A fitly born and bred race ... would ... find it enough merely to live— and would ... in the fact of life itself discover and achieve happiness— *with Being suffused night and day by wholesome extasy*, surpassing all the pleasures that wealth, amusement, and even gratified intellect, erudition, or the sense of art, can give.[138]

Whitman's statement in the face of this, "I accept Time absolutely. / It alone is without flaw, it alone rounds and completes all," [139] could only mean that Whitman accepts time only as an important factor in the spiritual growth of mankind, but not in the absolute sense, as an ultimate value, as Mercer understands it.[140] For Whitman has, as a result of self-knowledge, gained that "being" which is ever full and self-contained in virtue of its own inherent properties and which, therefore, does not depend upon a process of growth, upon time to

[136] Holloway, *op. cit.*, pp. 714, f.

[137] "A Song for Occupations," 6.

[138] Holloway, *op. cit.*, p. 712. (Italics mine.) This ecstasy of eternal being is a constant and living experience to Thoreau. See *Walden*, chap. iv.

[139] "Song of Myself," 22.

[140] See Mercer, "Limitations in *Leaves of Grass*," *Vedanta and the West*, XII (January-February, 1949), 21–25.

"round and complete" it. With reference to himself he says that he (the poet) "is complete in himself."[141] "I am sufficient as I am."[142]

Similarly also Whitman's belief in the future. Whitman sees that the future is full of promise for the growth and fulfilment of the capacities of human beings, and for the accomplishment and materialization of his own prophecies—though, of course, his own life is fulfilled in the eternal present, and does not wait to be consummated at a future date. The following will make his standpoint clear. "I submit, therefore, that the fruition of democracy, on aught like a grand scale, resides altogether in the future,"[143] and, "the only large and satisfactory justification of it (democracy) resides in the future, mainly through the copious production of perfect characters among the people, and through the advent of a sane and pervading religiousness."[144] Hence, speaking of his faith in what the future may bring forth, he says, "Of men or states, few realize how much they live in the future . . . without it, there were little meaning in lands or poems—little purport in human lives."[145] Vedanta too accedes as much. Time is an important factor in spiritual life. It is through a process of rectification of our wrong views that we attain the power of discrimination. Prajapati in Chhandogya Upanishad, 8.7.12, instructs Indra progressively in the nature of the *atman*. Bhrigu Varuni in the Taittiriya (3.1) rises progressively from the planes of matter, life, mind, consciousness, to the plane of bliss and realizes that to be the *brahman*. In the view of Vedanta time is unreal in the sense that the absolute is not in time; but in the phenomena we can afford to have time process. Whitman like a true Vedantin accepts time only in a relative sense and finds it valuable in preparing men for the supreme realization of immortality.

It is, however, true that time and space exercise a certain fascination over Whitman: "the beginningless, endless wonder Time—the other wonder Space."[146] In his self-expansion Whitman transcends the bounds of time and space; he "competes with, outcopes space and time."[147] For him they are merged into a vast spiritual continuum or

141 Holloway, *op. cit.*, p. 574.
142 "One Hour to Madness and Joy," in "Children of Adam."
143 Holloway, *op. cit.*, p. 685.
144 *Ibid.*, p. 688.
145 *Ibid.*, p. 733.
146 *Complete Writings*, Vol. VI, Part II, Note 175.
147 Holloway, *op. cit.*, p. 714.

expanse. The space and time of ordinary experience are displaced by spiritual space and time—which the dynamic self sees as symbols of dynamism. Spirit is time because it is ever creative; spirit is space because it is all-embracing and ever-expansive. Time is symbolic of creation, space of expansion. Space attracts Whitman's imagination because of its expansiveness:

> O to realize space!
> The plenteousness of all, that there are no bounds,
> To emerge and be of the sky, of the sun and moon and flying clouds, as one with them.[148]

"Thou matest time, smilest content at Death, / And fillest and swellest full the vastness of Space."[149] Hence it is that he shows a constant preoccupation with time and space and accepts them as eternal ties,

> Till when the ties loosen,
> All but the ties eternal, Time and Space,
> Nor darkness, gravitation, sense, nor any bounds bounding us.
> Then we burst forth, we float,
> In Time and Space O soul! prepared for them,
> Equal, equipt at last, (O joy! O fruit of all!) them to fulfil O soul.[150]

The idea of transmigratory existence also holds a certain appeal to his imagination because of its dynamism: "Myself moving forward then and now and forever."[151]

> We have thus far exhausted trillions of winters and summers,
> There are trillions ahead, and trillions ahead of them,
> Births have brought us richness and variety,
> And other births will bring us richness and variety.[152]

Newer births mean richer and varied self-expression. But this transmigratory movement is purely a dynamic movement and hence it is "motiveless."[153] It is in the field of dynamic activity only and does not detract from the original state of the self as pure, real existence. For, when the soul realizes its true essence, immortality, and dis-

---

[148] "A Song of Joys." Cf. Brihadaranyaka, 1.4.10. Vamadeva in his self-opening began to feel that he was Manu and Sun.

[149] "Passage to India," 8.

[150] "Darest Thou Now O Soul," in "Whispers of Heavenly Death."

[151] "Song of Myself," 32.

[152] *Ibid.*, 44.

[153] To the unenlightened reincarnation offers spiritual opportunities; to the knower, of course, *karma* and rebirth as such will be meaningless.

engages itself from the ties of materiality—the very knowledge of its immaterial and essential nature saves it from the effects of material existence. Whitman possesses this saving knowledge; he knows that his essential nature is indestructible and, therefore, separate from the processes by which it becomes embodied. "O to disengage myself from these corpses of me, which I turn and look at where I cast them, / To pass on, (O living! always living!) and leave the corpses behind,"[154] and, "I absolve you from all except yourself spiritual bodily, that is eternal, you yourself will surely escape, / The corpse you leave will be but excrementitious."[155] Transmigration sullies him who has desires and who seeks their fulfilment through endless births. Desire is the root of transmigratory existence. The knower of the self who, having risen above ego-consciousness, has rooted out his desire, and renounced all contact with actions and their fruits, is freed from transmigration, and becomes immortal in this very life.[156]

Consistently with the dynamic phase of the self, Whitman speaks of "eternal progress" and of a development that has no stoppage.[157]

> Ever the dim beginning,
> Ever the growth the rounding of the circle,
> Ever the summit and the merge at last, (to surely start again)
> Eidólons! eidólons![158]

The dynamic phase is one of perpetual enrichment, greater and greater enlarging of consciousness, and newer and vaster fields for the expansive activity of the spirit, "always changing, advancing, retreating, enlarging, condensing, widening, being wafted to spirituality."[159] But this dynamic activity cannot change or conflict with the real, transcendent nature of the self as pure being and immutable substance. In Whitman spiritual dynamism and consciousness of the eternal being exist hand in hand. Whitman does not seek through the dynamic expansion any further fulfilment for his own self. He is ever conscious of his fulness and self-completion. He exists as he is and sits content.

154 "O Living Always, Dying Always," in "Whispers of Heavenly Death." Cf. Gita, 2.22.
155 "To One Shortly to Die," in "Whispers of Heavenly Death."
156 See Brihadaranyaka, 4.4.5, 6, 7 and Sankara's commentary.
157 "Starting from Paumanok," 2. "There is no stoppage and never can be stoppage," "Song of Myself," 45.
158 "Eidólons," in "Inscriptions."
159 *Complete Writings*, Vol. VI, Part II, No. 26.

This internal dynamism is, however, purely the result of the release from all constraining elements and the opening of the wider self.

> O the joy of my spirit—it is *uncaged*, it darts like lightning!
> It is not enough to have this globe or a certain time,
> I will have thousands of globes and all time.[160]

This expansion of the dynamic being yields the experience of the cosmic self and opens out the cosmic and the supercosmic intuitions. The supercosmic intuition is the apprehension of the formless. The Upanishads, too, conceive of a kind of spiritual dynamism, but they make it clear that the highest reality is the formless absolute, the spirit-in-transcendence, and that it can only be apprehended in the silence of transcendence, not in expression and "meditation" on the concrete. The thrill and exultation of the vital, dynamic self, the activism of the creative spirit, is followed by an in-drawing of consciousness and self-immersion.

Whether Whitman attained this transcendence or not is a moot point. In Mercer's opinion this final transcendence was not consummated for Whitman. He "becomes absorbed in the spiritually concrete at the expense of the spiritually transcendent," and loses himself in enhanced life.[161] We may, however, discover in Whitman's later writings some suggestions and hints which lead us to believe that Whitman in his later years experienced transcendence. The postwar years witnessed a definite inward change in the poet. Referring to his later poems, Whitman writes, "I end my books with thoughts, or radiations from thoughts, on death, immortality, and a free entrance into the spiritual world."[162] The very fact that Whitman in his later years begins to sing more and more of death and the "unseen soul" is indicative of such a change in him, a ripening of spirit and a tendency to grow increasingly introverted. Critics have noticed an Indian summer atmosphere in "Specimen Days,"[163] The days he passed in the stillness and solitude of Timber Creek revealed the poet living in a

---

[160] "A Song of Joys."

[161] Mercer, "Limitations in *Leaves of Grass*," *Vedanta and the West*, XII (January-February, 1949), 21–25, XII (May-June, 1949), 82–87. M. N. Sircar is also of the opinion that Whitman's cosmical "I," like Vamadeva's vision, is only a cosmic vision not supercosmic. See *Hindu Mysticism: According to the Upanishads* (London: Kegan Paul, French, Trubner & Co., Ltd., 1934), pp. 124–27.

[162] Holloway, *op. cit.*, pp. 730 f.

[163] See *Whitman Handbook*, p. 221.

quiet resignation and the most satisfying repose of life—much in the manner of Thoreau by Walden Pond. The "Nature Notes"[164] bespeak a growing inwardness in the poet. It is as if he were escaping into the formless, the unknown. The tone of the following is unmistakable.

> This is thy hour O soul, thy free flight into the wordless,
> Away from books, away from art, the day erased, the lesson done,
> Thee fully forth emerging, silent, gazing, pondering the themes thou
>      lovest best,
> Night, sleep, death and the stars.[165]

The poem, "Halcyon Days" further suggests that after a career of expansive activity Whitman's soul was craving for eternal rest, that Whitman had really begun to experience the blessedness and peace that always crown and consummate a life of action and dynamism:

> Not from successful love alone,
> Nor wealth, nor honor'd middle age, nor victories of politics or war;
> But as life wanes, and all the turbulent passions calm,
> As gorgeous, vapory, silent hues cover the evening sky,
> As softness, fulness, rest, suffuse the frame, like freshier, balmier air,
> As the days take on a mellower light, and the apple at last hangs really
>      finish'd and indolent-ripe on the tree,
> Then for the teeming quietest, happiest days of all!
> The brooding and blissful halcyon days!

And he feels the poise and tranquility that accompany the completion of a task; after experiencing the exquisite thrill of creation, he begins to enjoy the symphony of silence:

> The soothing sanity and blitheness of completion,
> The pomp and hurried contest—glare and rush are done;
> Now triumph! transformation! jubilate![166]

and,

> After the dazzle of day is gone,
> Only the dark, dark night shows to my eyes the stars;
> After the clangor of organ majestic, or chorus, or perfect band,
> Silent, athwart my soul, moves the symphony true.[167]

[164] See *Complete Writings*, Vols. I, II.
[165] "A Clear Midnight" (1881), in "From Noon to Starry Night."
[166] "An Ended Day," in "Good-Bye My Fancy."
[167] "After the Dazzle of Day," in "Sands at Seventy."

In "Democratic Vistas," too, and other prose pieces of this later period we come across further suggestions of this growing "inwardization." There is a clear emphasis here on "interior consciousness," on the soul and its solitary broodings. This passage from the "Vistas" is a sure testimony to the new elevation Whitman was undergoing during these years.

> Alone, and identity, and the mood—and the soul emerges, and all statements, churches, sermons melt away like vapors. Alone, and silent thought and awe, and aspiration—and then the interior consciousness, like a hitherto unseen inscription, in magic ink, beams out its wondrous lines to the sense. Bibles may convey, and priests expound, but it is exclusively for the noiseless operation of one's isolated self, to enter the pure ether of veneration, reach the divine levels, and commune with the unutterable.[168]

Whitman here shows a deeper appreciation of the value of inwardness and depth in preference to expansion and enrichment. The highest path of spiritual life is the path of inwardness, where the soul sinks down into itself and apprehends the self in the self and alone through the self (*ātmani ātmānam ātmanā*) without turning its vision upon the outward world. The poet of *élan vital*, of "life immense in passion, pulse, and power"[169] seems for the moment to retire into the isolation of his soul. The dynamics of the soul which cried, "Wider and wider they spread, expanding, always expanding, outward and outward and forever outward,"[170] is followed by withdrawal and self-centripetence.[171] "*Retire within thyself*", he wrote down in his manuscript.[172] "Mask with the lids thine eyes O soul! Droop-droop thine eyes O soul. Be not abased. I sing the unaccomplished—I sing the vast dark unknown. . . . Then chant (celebrate) the unknown, the future hidden spiritual world, the real reality." Then follows a poem which has very great significance in this connection:

> Mask with their lids thine eyes, O soul!
> Pass to the unaccomplished, over the vast unknown
> Droop, droop thine eyes O soul

[168] Holloway, *op. cit.*, p. 693.
[169] "One's-Self I Sing," in "Inscriptions."
[170] "Song of Myself," 45.
[171] "Centripetal isolation of a human being in himself," Holloway, *op. cit.*, p. 687.
[172] See *Whitman's Workshop*, n. 14, pp. 190–91.

Exalt thyself to musing—speed thy flight—thy slough dropt from
thee
The standards of the light and sense shut off
To darkness now retiring
Aloof inward to thy abysms
How curious then appears the world
Thy comrades, life and this thy visage, passive each
The objective world behind thee left.[173]

Whitman also realized that living experience is more important
than self-expression. Might it not, after all, be that the best has remained unexpressed?

After the countless songs, or long or short, all tongues, all lands,
Still something not yet told in poesy's voice or print—something
lacking,
(Who knows? the best yet unexpress'd and lacking.)[174]

The strange sense began pressing in upon him that the *Leaves* for
which he lived and worked was but a futile attempt at self-expression.[175] The urge for expression is a limitation on the soul; creation
itself is seen as a delusive activity when the soul enters the higher
regions. Even the world of solid things and materials seems to "fall
apart and vanish."

A vague mist hanging 'round half the pages:
(Sometimes how strange and clear to the soul,
That all these solid things are indeed but apparitions, concepts, non-
realities?)[176]

The suggestions in these lines are unmistakable. Whether these
visions were to Whitman anything more than intermittent glimpses
should, however, remain a matter for speculation. Nevertheless, in
his writings the relative and the concrete receive greater emphasis, and

[173] *Ibid.*, This MS is not dated. But, regardless of the date of its composition,
the poem clearly suggests that Whitman had unmistakable glimpses into the region
of transcendence. Emory Holloway relates of Whitman that "in June 1888 Whitman one day drove to the river to watch the setting sun. Lost in reverie he remained
motionless till thoroughly chilled by the damp of evening," *Walt Whitman :
An Interpretation in Narrative* (New York: Alfred A. Knopf, 1926), p. 311.
[174] "The Unexpress'd," in "Good-Bye My Fancy."
[175] "These toils and struggles of baffled impeded articulation," *Complete
Writings*, IX, 17.
[176] "Apparitions," in "Good-Bye My Fancy."

Whitman remains to the last preoccupied with time, change, and evolution and accepts the relative values of love and comradeship. Though Whitman is ever conscious that he is a liberated soul himself, he refuses to flee from the world into pure contemplation. He has in him the cosmic consciousness fully developed, but he deliberately sets himself against being mastered by it.[177] "The physical and the sensuous, in themselves or in their immediate continuations, retain holds upon me, which I think are never entirely releas'd; and those holds I have not only denied, but hardly wish'd to weaken."[178]

Our analysis of Whitman's thought reveals a striking kinship with the Vedantic philosophy in respect to all outstanding metaphysical questions. No doubt Whitman was attracted to the German philosophical ideas, probably later in his life, and his references to Kant, Fichte, Schelling, and Hegel reveal a fairly clear understanding of their systems. He even described himself as "the greatest poetical representative of German philosophy." But, as has been observed, there are significant temperamental differences between him and the Germans of which he himself was not wholly unaware. Nevertheless, there are certain features of these German philosophers which account for Whitman's attraction to them. There is, for instance, the evolutionary dynamism of the German idealists, which might have been congenial to his temperament. The conclusion that the universe is a rational order—which, no doubt, is the common principle of all rationalist philosophies—and that everything in it is evolving systematically offers intellectual support to Whitman's faith in the "moral unity and sanity of the creative scheme,"[179] In Hegel's system becoming, or development, is only a movement of categories, not a historical process, and all things in it are eternally realized and fixed.[180] But, notwithstanding this, his doctrine provides a genuine basis for a philosophy of development. In the Hegelian dialectic could be seen a formula for America's dynamic growth. Whitman was impressed with the idea of "the endless process of creative thought . . . the whole mass of everything steadily, unerringly tending and flowing toward the permanent utile and morale as rivers to oceans."[181] Hegel's conception

[177] See Bucke, *op. cit.*, p. 232.
[178] Holloway, *op. cit.*, p. 729.
[179] Holloway, *op. cit.*, p. 788.
[180] See McTaggart, *op. cit.*, chap. v.
[181] Holloway, *op. cit.*, p. 787.

that history is the manifestation of the spirit, and a dialectical process in which contradictions are progressively resolved, producing good out of struggle and conflict,[182] justified Whitman's intuitive faith in universal good and harmony, and his hope for American democracy. The comprehensiveness of Hegel's interpretation, embracing in its compass all phases and aspects of life, the moral and material purposes —history, politics, science, and religion—and showing them to be necessary phases of the world process, contributing their part to the general progress of humanity, was also significant to Whitman. He needed some justification for these, since his spiritual democracy itself was to develop in conformity with modern civilization. Hegel had shown that political and social institutions and all historical events are the necessary processes by which the absolute attains self-expression.

> In my opinion the above formulas of Hegel are an essential and crowning justification of New World democracy in the creative realms of time and space. There is that about them which only the vastness, the multiplicity and the vitality of America would seem able to comprehend, to give scope and illustration to, or to be fit for, or even originate.[183]

There is little doubt that German idealism profoundly impressed Whitman's mind, though it is difficult to ascertain what part it played in the origin of his ideas. Whitman noted: "Taking their whole philosophy it is the most important emanation of the mind of modern ages and of all ages because it assumes to answer and does answer the deepest questions of the soul, of identity." It is not quite clear, however, that Whitman fully realized that certain implications of German thought conflicted with some of his basic beliefs. It is more likely that he understood the German dialectics rather as a symbolic expression of the dynamics of his own spirit than that he grasped its fullest theoretical implications.[184]

The foregoing study of Whitman has been suggested not, certainly, as the only method of interpreting him, but as one that may often yield

---

[182] See "Roaming in Thought" (After Reading Hegel), in "By the Roadside."

[183] Holloway, *op. cit.*, pp. 788, f.

[184] In a footnote to No. 175, *Complete Writings*, Vol. VI, Part II, treating of the German philosophers, the editors comment: "Throughout 175, as in all Whitman's writings, the hands may be the hands of Esau (Hegel, Schelling, etc.), but the voice is always the voice of Jacob—Whitman himself."

the full depth of his meanings. The unity of thought and experience in his poetry calls for a consistent and unified interpretation. The Vedantic doctrine, in my opinion, provides such a unified standpoint from which a large bulk of Whitman's poetry and prose may be profitably studied. A major hurdle to a full understanding of *Leaves of Grass* is the problem of interpreting the meaning of their lines, some of which still remain obscure and esoteric. Whitman's poems have lent themselves to an extreme diversity of interpretation, sometimes even to contradictory interpretations, which perhaps is a measure of the richness of their implication. But no interpretation can, in my opinion, do full justice to Whitman if it does not take into account the central concept of self around which the poet's meanings are woven. The standpoint that is steadily employed in this study is, of course, a purely philosophical one; a certain theory of consciousness and reality that is known as Advaita Vedanta. Modern criticism has constantly applied non-literary techniques and bodies of knowledge to gain insights into works of literature. Literary criticism is a multi-pronged attack on the problem of meaning as embodied in a work. In interpreting Whitman in the light of Hindu mysticism I have also tried to clear certain common misconceptions about Vedantic idealism and Whitman's own position in relation to it. Such, for instance, is the misconception that Whitman is not a thoroughgoing idealist like the Vedantist and that his essentially dynamic nature is in opposition to the latter's static viewpoint. Such also is the opinion that Brahminical mysticism seeks fulfilment through self-obliteration and that its concept of Brahman leads to the depreciation of the individual. But as I have shown, the Vedantic conception is essentially a dynamic vision like Whitman's own and admits of a phase of dynamic activity in its cyclic course from self-emergence, through cosmic expansion, to a final return to its own center. But though, thus, this dynamism is the essence of Whitman's poetic vision, it is a purely symbolic activity, and is in the inner realms of the mind. Its engagement with the outer reality is a certain exercise of the spirit, free from the encumbrance of the worldly ties. These and other aspects of Whitman's poetry are defined and illumined for us by these comparisons with the dynamic "I" envisioned in the apocalyptical verses of the Upanishads.

# Index

NOTE: For Whitman's untitled prose and notes see *Complete Writings* and *Walt Whitman's Workshop*.

171